HILARITY

by Allison Page

Hilarity

by Allison Page
Copyright © 2015 by Allison Page
All rights reserved

Published by EXIT PRESS

The premiere of Hilarity was produced by DIVAfest with support from the Theatre Bay Area CA$H grant program and the Dramatist Guild Fund.

Book design by Richard Livingston
Cover design by Sam Bertken
Cover photo and author photo by Natali Truax

CAUTION: Professionals and amateurs are hereby warned that all plays represented in this book are subject to a royalty. They are fully protected under the copyright laws of the United States of America, and of all countries covered by the International Copyright Union (including the Dominion of Canada and the rest of the British Commonwealth), and of all countries with which the United States has reciprocal copyright relations. All rights, including professional, amateur, motion picture, recitation, lecturing, public reading, radio broadcasting, television, and the rights of translation into foreign languages, are strictly reserved.

For performance inquiries, contact hilarity.play@gmail.com

For additional information about
EXIT PRESS, go to
www.exitpress.org

Paperback ISBN: 978-1-941704-05-9

EXIT PRESS
156 Eddy Street
San Francisco, CA 94102-2708
mail@theexit.org

First Edition: February 2015

For all the funny people.

Introduction

I have a vivid memory of Allison Page in a green tutu, red fez hat, bear ears and a black dot on her nose. Her voice growls out the sad and humorous story of a dancing bear drowning his lonely sorrows in beer. Allison bellowed and danced and drank as she performed surrounded by patrons at a bar who were a mix of hip young San Francisco good-time seekers and her fellow writers and performers. When she eventually knocked the last of the beer back and sank as the bear into a sleep that will bring death, the audience cheered wildly. BEEEEEEAARR was written by Megan Cohen and directed by Meg O'Connor, but it was the forceful woman with the startling blue eyes, carefully styled black hair, and wry wit that brought the suicidal dancing bear roaring to life.

Cyd, HILARITY's sardonic central character, isn't far removed from that dancing bear. Cyd is described in the play as "anarchy with tits", a force of nature that violently barrels through the structured lives of those around her with self-destructive carelessness. In so many ways Cyd is as different from Allison as night from day, but what makes her undeniably a creation of Allison's is the tension between the performer personality that is driven to make other people laugh and the private person that feels the pressures of reality like a collapsing building all around them.

"Oh, so you are a comedian. Be funny."

A comedian never works with a fourth wall, so there is a temptation to believe that they are always "on" and that their performances are available on demand. But much like prodding a sad dancing bear, a creature can only be pushed so far before they forget why they are dancing. Allison is not Cyd, but she's seen Cyd's shadow in the eyes of fellow comedians and performers and friends and family her whole life. When we sat down for the first time to talk about producing HILARITY she spoke about her deep interest in writing to explore the feelings of isolation, the desperate fear of irrelevance, and alcoholism that pervades the community she so dearly loves.

Then, almost a year to the day that Allison asked me to direct HILARITY, Robin Williams died. Ethan Hawk said in an interview about Robin Wiliams: "It didn't come for free."

It doesn't come for free. To be a mirror for life, for the pain and the anger; to juxtapose the abuses that a normal human must face even as they trudge through the trappings of absurd normalcy doesn't come for free. To speak a deeper truth while laughing at the ridiculous doesn't come for free.

HILARITY is funny. Brutally and devilishly funny. It is also sad and scary and angry. It couldn't be one without the other. These things are tied to each other intimately. But what Allison writes is also a play that is full of hope. The realities of recovery are dark and twisting and aching, but also full of renewal.

— Claire Rice
San Francisco
2015

This play came about from a love of some things and a fear of others. On the love side: comedians, snarky comebacks, pastrami sandwiches, chaos, and complex relationships. On the fear side: manipulators, enablers, violence, lack of self control, misplaced rage, co-dependency, substance abuse, and complex relationships. So it's a big bunch of fun - sometimes. Cyd is often a nightmare version of myself; the things I fear I could do or become if given the exact wrong set of opportunities. I think we all have nightmare selves. Hopefully yours doesn't make any of the decisions Cyd makes, but if they do I won't hold it against you. Everyone's got some chaos in them somewhere.

— Allison Page

HILARITY

Characters

CYD – (F) Pushing 30. A comedian with a serious drinking problem. Talented, haunted, unpredictable.

LIZ– (F) 24, Cyd's personal assistant. Dedicated, caring, slightly mousy – all the things Cyd isn't.

SOME GUY – (M) 25-35 Cyd's match in violence and manipulation.

SANDY – (M or F) 40+ Cyd's manager. Comic relief and a detached sensibility.

DEB – (F) 45+ Cyd's mom. A major contributor to Cyd's troubled personality. Delusional.

*Character note: SANDY was written as a non-gender-specific role, intended for whomever best fit the play at the time of production. In this version of the script, the pronoun "she" is used. This is due to the fact that this is the working script from the first production, with Jennie Brick originating the role. Changes to the pronoun based on the actor are perfectly acceptable, along with a change in reference in Act II Scene 1 when SANDY makes a comment about "my ex husband", which can be changed to "ex wife" in the event that there is a male identifying actor in the role and you deem SANDY to be more likely to have a wife than a husband. Or keep it husband and make that choice.

Settings

Cyd's New York City studio apartment.

The stage of an open mic night in a run down bar.

Production History

HILARITY was first produced by DIVAfest and was performed at EXIT Theatre in San Francisco from March 5th through March 28th, 2015 and was directed by Claire Rice.

The cast and crew were as follows:

Cyd: *Allison Page*
Liz: *Heather Kellogg*
Sandy: *Jennie Brick*
Some Guy: *Jason Pienkowski*
Deb: *Marie O'Donnell*

Assistant Director: *Sam Bertken*
Fight Choreographer: *Jon Bailey*
Lighting Designer: *Beth Cockrell*
Stage Manager: *Linda Huang*
Production Manager: *Teresa Hernandez*

ACT I

SCENE 1

A sparsely furnished studio apartment in New York City. It might have been nice once but a clear lack of care for the space in the last few years has caused it to gather a visible layer of dirt. There is a refrigerator with no magnets on it, a small side table with an old, plain lamp whose lamp shade is more than a little crooked, a slightly larger table DR topped with mostly-empty bottles of liquor, and a mattress in the middle of the floor. A bucket sits UC. CYD is sleeping on the mattress with a sheet, blanket, and pillow. She wears only a T-shirt and one boot. There are glasses, liquor bottles, a two liter of bloody mary mix, cups, ashtrays, half eaten bags of potato chips, and various pieces of trash littered on the floor around the mattress. A small wooden stool provides the only available seating apart from the mattress.

CYD stirs and groans.

CYD

Son of a bitch.

She slowly sits up, crushingly hungover.

Son of all the bitches.

She continues to groan, and considers whether or not she's about to be sick. She decides that she is, and crawls over to the bucket, throwing up into it.

Well, that was awful.

She looks into the bucket— it's disgusting. She looks around the room for a place to put it. She grabs the bucket and stows it in the refrigerator. Out of sight— out of mind. Somewhere, her cell phone rings. She tears through the apartment until she finds the phone in a shoe.

Yeah?

She clears her throat and grabs the two liter of bloody mary mix.

No, I'm fine.

She takes a swig of the bloody mary mix, swishes it around in her mouth, and swallows.

Uh-huh. Ya know, you should just call Liz about that stuff. I don't—

uh— have my calendar handy. Mostly because I don't own a calendar.
>   *She laughs and coughs a little.*

Sandy. Saaaaandy— c'mon. Yeah, just call Liz. Yeah, yeah, bye.
>   *There is a knock at the door. CYD starts to put on some pants. She is still zipping them up when LIZ enters. She is 24 and in many ways CYD's opposite. She carries a fairly large purse.*

Would it kill you to knock?

LIZ

I did knock.

CYD

Would it kill you to wait for me to answer the fucking door?

LIZ

It probably would kill me. Someone would find my decomposing corpse lying in the hall.

CYD

Wait, in this scenario, have I somehow managed to not leave my apartment for enough time that you start to actually rot?

LIZ

Yes, I think that's pretty clearly what I was going for there.

CYD

That's actually fucking sound logic.

LIZ

You should lay off the swearing. I just got off the phone with Sandy.

CYD

I just got off the phone with Sandy.

LIZ

She called me before she called you, thinking you probably wouldn't answer the phone. I'm surprised she called you at all.

CYD

I'm not that unreliable. You guys make me sound like … some fuckin' unreliable person.

LIZ

The swearing— the swearing.

CYD

I know!

LIZ

Dan's show is on basic cable.

CYD

Blech.

LIZ

You can't be dropping F-bombs on basic cable or they'll cut you off or cut you out of the show and go to a video of a cute kitten.

CYD

Speaking of cute things, money is adorable— do you have some for me?

LIZ

(sighing) Yeah. Maybe don't spend it all in one day. I don't even know why I'm bothering to say that because I know that you will, but I guess it just makes me feel better for trying to prevent it.

    LIZ starts to hand CYD some cash, but pulls it away.

LIZ

But you have to do something for me this time.

CYD

No, I hate doing things.

LIZ

Promise and I'll give you your allowance: a sentence I never thought I'd utter to an adult.

CYD

I don't even know what I'm promising.

LIZ

Yes, that's how this works.

    Eventually CYD snatches the money out of her hand.

CYD

So what do you want?

LIZ

I got you something.

CYD

Like ... a present? Is it digestible?

LIZ takes an e-cigarette out of her purse.

LIZ

I want you to use this ... it's an e-cigarette.

CYD takes it.

CYD

What sorcery is this?

LIZ

It's better for you. It's just vapor. It doesn't have all that lung-blackening stuff in it.

CYD

I hate this.

LIZ

You haven't even used it yet.

CYD

It's like a skinny robot penis.

LIZ

You charge it and refill it. And it doesn't smell or anything.

CYD

You know what else everybody thought was really great? Painting watch faces with radium. Everybody's happy until Betty's face starts melting off.

LIZ

Just try it. You've had worse things in your body.

CYD

I cannot argue with that. Fine, who cares, I'll take it. Did I tell you Sharon was on Letterman last week?

LIZ

Oh, here we go.

CYD

I was on Letterman, ya know.

LIZ

No, you weren't.

CYD

No, I wasn't.

LIZ

Because they cut you out of the episode.

CYD

Yeah, well, they did the same thing to Bill Hicks so I'm in good company. I was just too edgy for 'em.

LIZ

No, you were cut out because Dave didn't like your attitude backstage when he ran into you in the hallway and you tried to tell him how to do his job. Also you sound really arrogant when you compare yourself to Bill Hicks, you know that right?

CYD

Oh you call him Dave now? You guys are best friends?

LIZ

Doesn't everyone call him Dave?

CYD

I have no idea. And he's no Johnny Carson, anyway.

LIZ

You could always just wait around for Johnny Carson to call you, if you're unwilling to stoop to Dave's level ... or actually Dan's level, since Dave is now out of the question for the foreseeable future.

CYD

Johnny Carson is dead.

LIZ

Exactly. So don't screw this up.

CYD

Dave'll come back around. You'll see. And I can work clean if I have to—

LIZ

You have to.

CYD

Okay, so I fuckin' will!

LIZ

Okay, great! *(beat)* You smell bad.

CYD

You always come bearing tidings of great joy, don't you?

LIZ

Were you out last night?

CYD

No, I stayed home to knit a sweater. It's got a panda on it.

LIZ

Did you do a set somewhere or did you just go to the bar?

CYD

What's it to you what my panda sweater and I are doing?

LIZ

You have to choose your best material for Dan's show—

CYD

Dan's show on basic cable.

LIZ

—For Dan's show on basic cable. And right now all your stuff is old. Everybody's already seen it and they're not going to tune in late on a Friday night to watch you tell five year old jokes.

CYD

Clinton isn't relevant anymore?

LIZ

Bill or Hillary?

CYD

I'm kidding. I've never had a Bill Clinton bit.

                    LIZ

Maybe you should get a Hillary bit.

                    CYD

I don't do politics. I should have some breakfast.

                    LIZ

It's PM.

                    CYD

Yup.

    She takes an aspirin with several large gulps of bloody mary mix.

Proceed.

                    LIZ

We should talk about that, too.

                    CYD

If you want to talk this much, I should get to lie down on a couch and cry.

                    LIZ

Think about eating some real food. You don't look healthy.

                    CYD

Maybe you should pump some wheatgrass directly into my eyeballs.

                    LIZ

Cyd—

                    CYD

(desperately changing the topic) Hey! I've been working on some new stuff!

                    LIZ

Oh good, what about?

                    CYD

You know the Sean Connery bit? Where he's the airline pilot?

                    LIZ

The one you've been working on for a year?

                              CYD

Yeah, that one. I think I've almost got it where I want it.

                              LIZ

Oh yeah?

                              CYD

Yeah, I think I need to have him say the word "descent". It just sounds good with the voice, like

   She affects a Sean Connery voice.

"We are now making our descent."

                              LIZ

(not laughing) That's funny.

                              CYD

I can tell. Ya know, by the laughter.

                              LIZ

Sorry.

                              CYD

God, I hate that. If you thought it was funny you'd just fucking laugh.

                              LIZ

Maybe it's not funny.

                              CYD

Maybe you're wrong.

                              LIZ

It's an opinion.

                              CYD

A wrong opinion.

                              LIZ

I can't have a wrong opinion, that's what makes it an opinion.

                              CYD

I bet you raised your hand a lot in class.

                              LIZ

I'm just tired. And it's not like you did the whole bit.

CYD

Yeah, whatever.

LIZ

You're going to work some stuff out tonight, right?

CYD

You're gonna need a pretty big Baby Bjorn. I have really heavy legs.

LIZ

I'm just checking. Sandy wanted me to check.

CYD

Great, you checked. You get a participation ribbon and Sandy gets a new pony.

LIZ

You're in a mood. I'm gonna go.

CYD finally gets up and follows LIZ.

CYD

Ah, I didn't mean anything by it. I just woke up, ya know?

LIZ

It's fine. I have to go, anyway. I just wanted to give you that stuff.

CYD

Ya want the rest of my bloody mary mix for the road?

LIZ

No thanks.

CYD

Give us a hug! Come on, I promise to take some vitamins.

LIZ

You're lying.

CYD

Yes, I am. But didn't that feel good for a second there?

CYD grabs hold of LIZ, who stands still.

LIZ

You're going to pick me up, aren't you?

                                    CYD

YEEEEES!

    CYD bear hugs LIZ, lifting her up.

                                    LIZ

Ugh, put me down!

                                    CYD

Never!

                                    LIZ

You smell like a nightmare!

                                    CYD

I know! Even now my filth is seeping into your very soul!

    CYD eventually puts LIZ down.

You're heavier than I remembered.

                                    LIZ

You're just weaker than you should be because you're not eating any vegetables. Remember vegetables?

                                    CYD

No. Tell me more.

                                    LIZ

They're green and they keep you alive.

                                    CYD

Ah yes. Weed and absinthe—

                                    LIZ

—Are not vegetables. Have a salad. I know you know what salad is.

                                    CYD

Says you.

                                    LIZ

Okay, I really have to get going. I'm probably already late.

                                    CYD

Where are you going? Are you late to high tea with the goddamn Queen of England? Because she seems pretty boring, if I'm being totally honest.

At least here you can count on some entertainment.

LIZ

And no toilet paper.

CYD

That might be true.

LIZ

I'm going to meet up with Clark.

CYD

Who the fuck is Clark?

LIZ

—Clark and I have been dating for two months. I know you know that.

CYD

Stop knowing what I know all the time. It's annoying.

LIZ

I know you know because I told you about him. More than once. Many times, actually.

CYD

I probably wasn't listening when you told me.

LIZ

Well, I'm telling you again.

CYD

Who says I'm listening now?

LIZ

I'll see you tomorrow. You have any laundry you need washed?

CYD

Nah, I'll just Febreeze it.

LIZ

You have Febreeze?

CYD

I have vodka?

LIZ

Promise me you'll go work out some new material, pretty please?

CYD

Yeah, yeah, I promise. Get outta here.

CYD opens the door for LIZ and shuts it when she's gone.

Clark. Who fuckin' names their kid Clark? Was he born wearin' a cape?

CYD sits on the stool facing the audience. She treats the audience like a mirror as she starts to practice impressions.

Okay, Sean. It's you and me.

The Sean Connery voice takes over.

Attention passengers, we are now making our descent. Descent. Desceeeeent. Overhead compartment. She sells seashells by the sea shore. I am in a League of Extraordinary Gentlemen. My beard is gray but I have a heart of spun gold.

Lights fade to black.

ACT I

SCENE 2

An open mic at a bar. CYD is standing center with a mic stand in front of her. She's comfortable with the mic she's holding, she looks like she's been holding it her entire life. But she's also drunk, and still drinking as she talks.

CYD

Anyway … It's a good thing this whole comedy situation has worked out. If this has actually worked out. I had an office job for about a week. The guy who sat next to me ate constantly and always sounded like he was consuming his last meal. He'd eat a peach and it sounded like a drowning whale sucking a juicy duplex through its baleen. *(She acts out this sound.)* So I killed him and hid the body in a malfunctioning fax machine … nobody really uses those anymore anyway. He's probably still there—faxing. Hey, ever feel like your soul was shriveling up like a Craisin in the sun?

She drinks.

That's not a joke, I was just wondering if anyone else felt like that.

She drinks again.

Not that I care how you feel. Or how I feel. Not that you should worry about me, I don't feel anything. I'm a husk.

SOME GUY

(yelling from the audience) Show us your tits!

CYD

Oh my goodness, Christmas came early.

SOME GUY

Shut up and show us your tits!

CYD

I think Roosevelt said that.

SOME GUY

You're not funny!

CYD

The real question is whether it was Teddy or the other one … who was the other one?

SOME GUY

Booooooo!

CYD

Dude. If you're trying to piss me off enough to drive me from this shitty, sticky Wednesday night bar open mic … god, what am I doing up here?

She takes a drink.

Ah, fuck it, what do I care? Come on up. Come here.

SOME GUY

What?

CYD

Take the stage, motherfucker.

SOME GUY

(laughing with drunken discomfort) Uhhhhh …

CYD

Come on up. Don't believe what you've heard. Whatever you may have been hearing. Probably nothing. Don't believe the nothing that you've heard. Just come up here. You can bring your drink. I won't promise not to drink it, but you can bring it if it makes you feel cozy.

He is still hesitating.

What's the worst that could happen? I don't have any power tools or anything.

SOME GUY

(cocky) Okay, if that's really what you want!

SOME GUY staggers up to the stage. They are fairly equally matched in the drunk department. They stand there looking at each other for a moment.

Well ... this is awkward.

He laughs riotously at his own quasi-joke.

CYD

Yeah. So, all right. Go ahead.

SOME GUY

What?

CYD

Go ahead. Tell some jokes. Be funny.

SOME GUY

Hey, I already got a job!

He laughs and drinks some more.

CYD

No, see, you interrupted my set, so now you have to take over— that's how this works. Didn't anyone tell you? Lenny Bruce sent down that decree from the disappointing heavens and now we all must follow it. Not my fault. I was gonna talk about Hillary Clinton. So that's your topic. Hillary Clinton— go.

SOME GUY

Hillary Clinton is a bitch ... and so are you! HAHAHA!

CYD

Cupping her hands around her mouth.

Show us your tits! SHOW US YOUR TIIIIIITS!

SOME GUY

Fuck you.

CYD

No, fuck you.

SOME GUY

No, fuck you.

CYD

No, fuck you.

SOME GUY

No, fuck you.

CYD

… Abbott and Costello just aren't what they used to be.

SOME GUY

Who?

CYD

Look, this has been a real hoot. Unfortunately, I hate you. If you could get the hell out of here, that would be great.

SOME GUY

Whatever.

CYD

Experiment's over. Go home and watch reruns of CSI Miami and jerk off every time David Caruso adjusts his sunglasses or whatever it is that you do with your free time.

SOME GUY

Fuck you.

CYD

Oh boy, let's not start that again.

SOME GUY

You're not funny, but your tits are okay.

CYD

So are yours.

CYD and SOME GUY eye each other for a moment. They both finish their drinks. CYD turns back to the audience.

Listen, I don't want to expose you guys to this personification of douchey nightmarish wonder any longer than you've already been ... exposed. So, I'm just gonna end it here. Thank you very much, I'm Cyd. Good night. Oh, I might be on fucking basic cable on a show I highly doubt you care about in a few weeks, but I have an equal chance of sleeping behind the bar on top of Josh-the-bartender's tragically fashionable messenger bag.

(shouting to the bartender) Isn't that right Josh?! Okay, fuck it. Good night.

CYD starts to leave. SOME GUY stands there for a moment, until CYD grabs his arm and takes him off with her.

ACT I

SCENE 3

CYD's apartment after the open mic. A lot of commotion comes from the door to the apartment. CYD and SOME GUY come crashing into the room. SOME GUY is carrying CYD, who has her arms around his neck and her legs wrapped around his waist. They are making out with drunken aggression and look like they could topple over at any moment. SOME GUY is stumbling partially because he's carrying CYD and partially because he's very drunk. They match each other that way. At some point CYD bashes a boombox, CD player, or some other outdated music player she got for free somewhere, and it begins to play loud music to which no one would ever want to have sex.

CYD

Over there! Take me over there, you stupid fuck.

SOME GUY stumbles over to a table with a bottle of whiskey on it. They continue to kiss although it is difficult. They run into things but keep going. CYD picks up the whiskey and pours a shot, she hands the glass to SOME GUY. He takes the shot as she takes a pull straight from the bottle. He puts the shot glass down when he's finished—CYD is still drinking from the bottle. She finally sets it back down and goes back to messily making out with him. He staggers, they knock some things over. She clumsily starts to take his shirt off which proves to be a difficult endeavor.

                             CYD

Oh, come on!

> *She finally gets his shirt off. She looks at him, drunkenly assessing her conquest.*

                             CYD

Yeah, I guess you'll do.

                          SOME GUY

Fuck off.

> *They kiss some more, then separate to remove their pants. They do this mostly without their hands, just stepping on them until they're off of their bodies— the drunk method. It is a slow process. Finally, she points at the mattress.*

                             CYD

Lie down!

                          SOME GUY

Yes, ma'am.

> *CYD grabs her jeans and digs around in the pockets.*

What the hell-

                             CYD

Just a sec.

> *CYD retrieves her e-cigarette from her jeans.*

                          SOME GUY

Seriously? Come-

                             CYD

Shhhhh, stop having opinions.

> *She crawls on top of him. He stays lying down. The light of the e-cigarette glows in the darkness.*

                          SOME GUY

Are you … are you smoking?

                             CYD

No, it's a mirage.

SOME GUY

Like in the desert?

CYD

Just like in the desert. Now shut your mouth unless you're going to use it for something.

SOME GUY

Yeah, okay.

Lights fade to black as the blue tip of the e-cigarette glows in the darkness.

ACT 1

SCENE 4

CYD's apartment, the morning after. CYD and SOME GUY are lying on the mattress. CYD crawls out of bed, oblivious to the body next to her.

CYD

Oh man.

She stumbles to the refrigerator and opens it. She sees the bucket of vomit. She closes the door, looks around and spots a bottle of bloody mary mix. She takes a few swigs then turns on some music. She starts dancing and/or lip syncing and/or playing air guitar. She's rockin' out pretty hard for someone who should be very hung over. She periodically takes swigs of bloody mary mix. Eventually SOME GUY is awakened by the ruckus she's causing.

SOME GUY

What are you, crazy?

CYD

AHHHH!

She turns off the music. She stares, trying to figure out if she knows him or not.

SOME GUY

Uh-

CYD

Oh yeah. You're the heckler.

SOME GUY

Yeah.

CYD

Did we have sex?

SOME GUY

Yeah.

CYD

I fucked a heckler.

SOME GUY

Slowly getting up.

I feel like shit.

He goes to the fridge and opens it.

Got anything to drink?

CYD

You're not gonna wanna look in there.

SOME GUY

Whoa-

CYD

But I've got some nice room temperature bloody mary mix over here if you're interested.

She looks at the bottle.

Good year, too.

SOME GUY

Still looking in the fridge.

Is that-

CYD

Yeah. Close the door, you're lettin' the smell out.

SOME GUY

That's disgusting.

>*He shuts the door.*

CYD

Oh, are we getting judge-y already this morning? Because if we are, your hair is stupid.

SOME GUY

>*Patting down his hair.*

Isn't it kind of early in the morning for jokes?

CYD

I'm not joking; your hair is stupid.

SOME GUY

Hey, I'm not a morning person either. You really don't have anything else to drink in here?

CYD

No, I really don't. Sorry, this isn't the Ramada.

>*CYD grabs a notebook and pen, and starts writing. She ignores SOME GUY.*

SOME GUY

What are you doing?

>*She doesn't respond.*

I said, what are you doing?

CYD

Writing.

SOME GUY

I can see that.

CYD

And yet you ask.

SOME GUY

What are you writing?

                        CYD

Bits.
                     SOME GUY

Bits?
                        CYD

Jokes. Material. Shit. Stuff. Things. Words.
                     SOME GUY

What are you writing about?

> *She doesn't respond.*

I said, what are you-
                        CYD

Not you.
                     SOME GUY

Are you like this all the time?
                        CYD

Yes.
                     SOME GUY

You bring some guy home with you and the next morning you treat him like a stranger?
                        CYD

You are a stranger. And usually they don't stay the night, so it's kind of a non-issue.
                     SOME GUY

What was I gonna do, wander home at 4am?
                        CYD

More shocking things have happened throughout the course of history. Ever heard of Jeggings?
                     SOME GUY

You can't expect a man to drunkenly wander into the street.
                        CYD

I do it all the time. Certainly would have avoided this conversation, anyway.

SOME GUY

Eventually.

So what are you writing about?

CYD

Nothing earth-shattering.

SOME GUY

C'mon! I'll tell you if it's funny or not.

This strikes an unhappy chord.

CYD

Finally! I've waited all these years, toiling away in dingy clubs and laundromats with stages in them, and all this time all I really needed was some heroic, hungover, dog-breathed dude who just can't seem to see himself out, to tell me what's funny. To untie me from the railroad tracks of life and throw me over his sweaty shoulder so we can run off into the distance and never look back knowing that now, finally, after all this time —my joke is funny because he made it so. As God is my witness, I'll never go hungry again.

SOME GUY

… So what's the joke?

CYD

It's about a tennis player with no elbows. He can never get tennis elbow.

SOME GUY

What?

CYD

Tennis players often get tennis elbow. But this guy has no elbows, see, so he can't get tennis elbow. So he's the ultimate tennis player.

SOME GUY

How does a person not have any elbows?

CYD

I don't know, he just doesn't. Born that way, I guess.

SOME GUY

That's not funny, that's just weird.

CYD

It's not a joke yet, it's just an idea. Remember how I didn't want to tell you, and then you wouldn't shut up about it? This is what you get: a no-elbow tennis player without a punch line. Happy now?

SOME GUY

I don't even think tennis elbow is necessarily caused by playing tennis. I think it's just a name.

CYD

It really doesn't matter.

SOME GUY

It should matter to you if you have a shitty joke.

CYD

I don't have shitty jokes. And if I did I still wouldn't believe you because what the fuck do you know?

SOME GUY

I'm just saying, you know, you should strive for excellence.

CYD

What is that— a Nike commercial? Isn't it a little early for heckling?

SOME GUY

I don't heckle.

CYD

Oh really?

SOME GUY

No, I just react honestly.

CYD

You're honestly a shithead.

SOME GUY

I'd appreciate it if you didn't make it sound like I'm a fucking idiot. Because I'm actually not. You wouldn't know that, but I'm actually not.

CYD

You're an idiot and I fucked you, so by definition …

                    SOME GUY

You really don't like me, do you?

                        CYD

I don't even know you. But so far it's not looking good, no. I live alone for a reason.

                    SOME GUY

Because you hate everyone or because everyone hates you?

                        CYD

Yes. Why are you still here?

                    SOME GUY

I'm hungover. I don't like to go places when I'm hungover. You have an answer for everything. It's fucking tiring. Why'd you even bring me here last night?

                        CYD

To discuss the varied effects of global warming on the wetlands. Or because I was drunk and you're a good looking asshole. Which one do you think it is?

                    SOME GUY

Hey, I was just as drunk as you were!

                        CYD

Nobody said you weren't.

                    SOME GUY

Okay, well I just wanted that on the record. And you don't know I'm an asshole. You don't know me.

                        CYD

Men get heckled all the time. Every night. Especially if there's booze. Women? Not so much. And if a woman does get heckled, it's usually by another woman, because a man heckling a woman looks like a degenerate prick, and generally is one. And they probably wouldn't mind— the degenerate pricks, I mean—except that if other women are present and know about the degenerate pricks' nature, they probably won't have sex with him which is all the degenerate prick really wants, anyway ... because he's a-

BOTH

Degenerate prick.

CYD

You're catching on.

SOME GUY

So I'm an asshole for not caring if the women in the audience think I'm an asshole?

CYD

Yeah, because that means it's an essential part of who you are— being a fucking jerk, I mean.

SOME GUY

I guess you like fucking jerks, then.

CYD

I gravitate toward my own, yeah.

SOME GUY

It's nice when you can figure someone out right away.

CYD

I'm glad you know how easy it is.

SOME GUY

I was talking about you.

CYD

You have me figured out? Fuck, finally. So who the hell am I?

SOME GUY

You're an attention whore but you want everyone to think you don't care if they notice you.

CYD

Oh God. Says the guy who has yet to leave my apartment and won't stop talking.

SOME GUY

You know I'm right.

CYD

Okay.

SOME GUY

You like to order people around, but you don't respect them if they listen to you.

CYD

Deep.

SOME GUY

What you really want is someone who will stand up to you.

CYD

Do I?

SOME GUY

You do.

CYD

And why do I want that?

SOME GUY

Because you want to be around people just like you.

CYD

Narcissism. Now you're onto something. We have a psychologist on our hands!

SOME GUY

You want to be manipulated like you manipulate others.

CYD

Mmm, now you're losing me.

SOME GUY

No, I'm not.

CYD

Okay.

SOME GUY

You really don't know yourself, do you?

CYD

What a stupid question.

                    SOME GUY

So consider it a statement.

                        CYD

Great. Who cares? Congratulations on your community college psych course.

                    SOME GUY

Not me. I just thought I'd tell you I can see through your bullshit.

                        CYD

Yeah, all right, because you've known me for like … all together—maybe two and a half hours? Most of which you were drunk for? This isn't a romantic comedy where you tell me everything "real" about myself and then I trip on something and you catch me and carry me off somewhere to meet your quirky relatives and then I use the wrong fork for the oysters and everyone laughs.

                    SOME GUY

I've been here longer than that.

                        CYD

Yeah, unconscious. Don't say you can analyze my shit through osmosis.

                    SOME GUY

I'm a very good judge of character.

                        CYD

Congratulations.

> *SOME GUY approaches CYD and places one hand on her throat, backing her up against a wall.*

                    SOME GUY

You know how they say children actually love and need discipline and thrive when they have it, and might be little fucking bastards without it and turn into big fucking bastards who suck shit as adults because no one ever told them how it is? That.

                        CYD

Fuck, you're tiresome.

> *He kisses her. She allows it.*

                              CYD

Interesting tactic ... okay, I got shit to do. Play time is over. Mama's done with the chokey choke.

> He doesn't budge.

                              CYD

Fine.

> She kicks him hard in the shin. Surprised, he releases her. She grabs his clothes and tosses them at him.

                              CYD

Don't let the door hit you in the douche on the way out.

> He doesn't budge.

                              CYD

This is the part where you leave.

> He throws his clothes back on the floor. CYD takes a handful of cash out of her jeans and counts some of it out. She hands it to him.

                              CYD

Here.

                           SOME GUY

What's this?

                              CYD

For a cab. And a little extra.

                           SOME GUY

A little extra?

                              CYD

Yeah, I don't know, for a sandwich or a pint of blood of the young— whatever you want.

                           SOME GUY

Like a tip? ... Did you just give me a tip?

                              CYD

I wouldn't say it's a tip, I just—

SOME GUY

I'm not a gigolo.

CYD

You weren't leaving so I figured ... I mean, when a bellhop doesn't leave in a movie it's because he's waiting for money, and not knowing what else to compare this to-

SOME GUY

You are a real gem, aren't you?

He walks toward her.

CYD

What are you doing?

He continues to approach her. When he gets within her range, she punches him in the face.

SOME GUY

Fuck!

He pushes her hard on the chest, repeatedly. She takes a step back each time. Eventually she backs into the sink.

CYD

Knock it off.

He laughs and shakes his head. He turns his back to her and put his pants on.

SOME GUY

You're crazy, you know that? Totally nuts.

CYD

(growling) I'm not crazy!

She yells out, runs, and jumps onto his back.

CYD

AHHHHHHHH!

SOME GUY

What the fuck?!

He stumbles and throws her off of his back and onto the mattress. He takes a step to walk away, and she grabs his ankle, bringing

him clumsily to the floor.

CYD

I win. And I'm not crazy.

She dusts her hands off and walks to the door.

You may go now.

He follows her, then suddenly pins her up against the wall, choking her.

SOME GUY

Who's winning now?

She is gasping for air and hitting the wall with her hands. Finally, she manages to hit the inside of his elbow, causing his arm to bend so she can reach him, and punches him in the face again. The second she does this, he punches her back. They separate, both breathing hard and holding their faces where they've been hit. They stare at each other, huffing and puffing like beasts. They stay in potential pouncing positions. Beat.

SOME GUY

This is really stupid.

CYD

We're just gonna do this all day. Nobody's gonna win.

SOME GUY

Uh, I would win, I'm bigger-

CYD

Do you need me to explain Jack and The Beanstalk right now?

SOME GUY

You mean David and Goliath?

CYD

Don't give yourself so much credit.

SOME GUY

I'm gettin' outta here.

CYD

Good idea.

> SOME GUY *grabs whatever remains of his stuff, and leaves.* CYD *goes to the freezer to find something cold to put on her face. The only thing in the freezer is a single serving frozen pizza. She sits on the mattress and holds the pizza to her face. She manages to find her e-cigarette and uses it with disdain for a moment. Then pours herself a drink of whatever is nearby. She tries to coordinate smoking, drinking, and holding a pizza on her face with some difficulty. A moment later the apartment buzzer goes off. She reluctantly gets up and pushes the buzzer.* SANDY *comes blowing in.*

SANDY

Cyd, baby, I've been calling you nonstop for hours. I know you think you're an artist, but you need to answer your phone. Since you haven't replied to any of my emails for the last three years, you could at least pick up when I call ya, or I'm going to have to get one of those messenger foxes and I really don't know where to get one in the city. Probably just get hit by a car when it's crossin' the street, anyway.

> SANDY *laughs at her own joke, as usual.* CYD *alternates smoking and drinking.* SANDY *sits beside her.*

SANDY

Geez, Cyd. A little early for that, dontcha think?

> *Beat.*

Ya left your door open, by the way.

> *Beat.*

So, how's the new material comin' along? Pretty good? 'Cause they're gonna be expecting new stuff. No Clinton jokes, ya know.

CYD

Why does everyone keep saying that?

SANDY

Just tryin' to keep you on the ball, Cyd. Now, you know there are certain things you can't say on TV, right? Just certain words that ya can't-

CYD

Jesus, Sandy. I know how to work clean.

SANDY

See, like there. You'd probably just leave off the Jesus part ... bible belt and whatnot. Ya know, it's on basic cable but sometimes stuff makes it on the YouTube.

CYD

I've been on TV before.

SANDY

Not for a while.

CYD

Why'd you say it like that?

SANDY

Like what? I'm just talking.

CYD

Like I'm gonna screw it up.

SANDY

Hey, I didn't say that! I just said, ya know, keep it clean. Squeaky clean.

CYD

You think my plan was just to run up there and yell "CUUUUUUNT! CUNT CUNT CUNT CUNT!" a million times? Sandy, I'm not stupid. What are you doing here, anyway?

SANDY

Just seeing how things are ... so how are things? How's everything?

CYD

How's everything? Everything's fine.

SANDY

Yeah?

CYD

Yeah.

SANDY

Are ya layin' off the uh-?

CYD

Sure.

SANDY

Yeah? Hey, that's great!

Hesitating.

So ... have ya seen Liz lately?

CYD

She was here yesterday.

SANDY

Was she?

CYD

Sure, why shouldn't she be? She's my assistant, isn't she? So she assists me?

SANDY

Just checking in.

CYD

I'm not a hotel.

SANDY

Laughing harder than is deserved.

Hey, that's funny!

CYD

Not really.

SANDY

Well, I thought it was funny.

CYD

Of course you did.

SANDY

A sudden attempt to be stern.

There's no need to be caustic with me, Cyd. Out of anyone in the world, there's no need to be caustic with me.

CYD does not respond. Beat. SANDY reverts back to regular SANDY.

SANDY

What are you workin' on?

CYD

I'm just going to get up there and say "I'm not a hotel," seventeen times in a row, since that's so hilarious.

SANDY

Aw, c'mon. What are you working on?

CYD

Some impressions and stuff. I have a bit of Sean Connery flying a plane.

SANDY

What else?

CYD

I don't fucking know, Sandy, okay? I'm not going to sit here and explain every little nugget of a thought to you. I'm just working on some things.

SANDY

You have three weeks. I'm just trying to make sure you pay attention to what's at stake here, Cyd.

CYD

At stake?

SANDY

Yeah. You know.

CYD

No, I don't know.

SANDY

I'm just saying you should make a real go of it. It's a paying gig, ya know. Those don't just drop right outta the sky!

CYD

Uh-huh.

SANDY

I'm just saying— money isn't a four letter word. All right. Well, I have to go. I have errands to run.

CYD

Fine by me.

                           SANDY

C'mere. Come on. Give old Pecan Sandy a hug.

> *SANDY embraces CYD, who is lazy and icy about it. SANDY holds CYD's face in her hands.*

                           SANDY

Hey, you can do this. You're the funniest freakin' person around if you wanna be. All right?

                            CYD

Yeah.

                           SANDY

All right.

> *Turning to exit.*

Maybe take a nap or something. You look like hell. I'll be seein' ya.

> *SANDY exits. CYD sits back down on the edge of the mattress. She finishes her drink and stares. Then she lies down on the mattress and falls asleep with the pizza on her face as the lights fade to black.*

ACT I

SCENE 5

> *Later the same day. CYD is lying in bed in the same clothes she had on before. The pizza is still on her face. There are a series of loud knocks on the door, then a pause, then LIZ enters.*

                            LIZ

You want me to knock, so I knock and you don't answer. Hilarious. Hey, are you sleeping?

> *She kneels down on the bed and taps on the pizza covering CYD's face.*

Wakey, wakey, eggs and bac-ey!

                            CYD

Ugh.

                            LIZ

Taking a nap, are we?

CYD

No we, just I.

LIZ

Even better. Wake up. You're always sleeping. I brought you a sandwich!

CYD

> *She sits up and removes the pizza from her face. A nasty bruise is beginning to form.*

Uh oh. What kind?

LIZ

Unicorn with mustard.

CYD

Looks like pastrami.

LIZ

They're very similar. Either way it has mustard.

> *CYD chuckles, shakes her head, and unwraps her sandwich. LIZ notices her face.*

LIZ

Holy shit. What happened to your face?

CYD

Hm? Oh. Uh. It was my fault. I overcooked my own steak. I like it medium rare, so I had to teach myself a lesson. This is what happens when you are your own housewife. But I've learned my lesson. Next time I'll get it right.

LIZ

God, you're weird. So, how's it going?

> *CYD shrugs and takes a bite of her sandwich. LIZ takes the pizza from her and puts it in the freezer.*

LIZ

How about I redecorate in here? And by "redecorate" I mean pick up some of this trash. Give it a bit less of a sidewalk feel. Upgrade it to a tiny warehouse feel.

CYD

Knock yourself out. Or don't. I only have one pizza and we have to wait for it to get cold again.

> *LIZ starts cleaning up the apartment while CYD continues to eat her sandwich.*

LIZ

On the way here, some guy on the sidewalk asked if I would sign his petition to ban ink pens worldwide. Said pencils are the future. I signed it. I figured—why not—ya know? It might be good karma or something. I mean, if I had a totally bogus petition, I'd want people to sign it.

> *CYD chuckles quietly. LIZ picks up something sharp and nicks her finger. She gasps.*

LIZ

Ah! Damn it!

CYD

Are you okay? What happened?

> *CYD jumps up.*

LIZ

I'm fine. I just cut my finger on your little broken glass collection over here.

CYD

Uhhh, hold on.

> *She runs off to the bathroom, and returns with a small hand towel. She wraps it around LIZ's finger.*

Sorry. I must have dropped a glass and forgotten to sweep it up.

LIZ

With your imaginary broom? It's okay, really. Pretty small cut. I'm just a gasper.

CYD

You sure you're okay?

LIZ

> *Unwrapping her finger a little.*

Definitely. See? No big deal. It's almost given up bleeding already. Go back to your sandwich.

CYD

If you say so.

> *CYD sits back down to eat her sandwich. LIZ nurses her wound for a moment, then goes back to cleaning.*

LIZ

Getting excited about the show? I am. Dan Lennon is kind of a hunk— if you're into middle-aged basic cable late night talk show hosts.

CYD

Yeah, I guess so.

LIZ

You're not nervous, are you?

CYD

Not really.

LIZ

You never are.

CYD

You know me. I haven't felt anything in years except the disappointment of my unfulfilled idealistic youth!

> *They both laugh. She's made this joke before. In the process of cleaning, LIZ has picked up several bottles of whiskey and assorted booze. She bundles them up and takes them off, presumably to the bathroom to dump them out in the sink. CYD watches her go into the bathroom with them. It takes her a moment to figure out what's going on.*

CYD

What are you doing with those?

LIZ

(*off*) Dumping them down the drain.

> *CYD jumps up to run after her.*

CYD

What the hell are you doing that for? Hey, that stuff isn't cheap!

> *LIZ comes back in, CYD right behind her, watching her like a hawk.*

LIZ

I assumed they were garbage, just lying around like that.

CYD

Well, they weren't.

LIZ

Oops. Sorry.

> *LIZ continues cleaning up around the apartment. CYD continues to watch her, suspiciously.*

CYD

I didn't know you were coming today.

LIZ

Oh yeah?

CYD

How is it that you happened to drop by just now?

LIZ

Just thought I'd see how you were doing.

CYD

Yeah that seems like a common theme lately.

LIZ

To check on how you were preparing for the show and everything.

CYD

Anything else?

LIZ

Hm?

CYD

Might there be some other reason you happened to be in the neighborhood, Liz?

LIZ

Nope. Now finish your sandwich.

CYD

I'm not hungry. And Sandy told you to come here.

                    LIZ

Did Sandy tell you that?

                    CYD

No. But that's what's going on, isn't it?

                    LIZ

Not everything is a conspiracy, Cyd.

                    CYD

Good old reliable Sandy sent you here to check up on me and take my fucking booze away.

                    LIZ

Oh, did she?

                    CYD

You know she did.

                    LIZ

If she did— and I'm not saying she did— what's so terrible about that?

                    CYD

It's mine. I own it. You can't just take my stuff away and dump it out.

                    LIZ

Well, I'm sorry.

                    CYD

That's fucked up.

> *She sits back down on the mattress to finish the sandwich.*

You can't just mess with other people's stuff.

                    LIZ

Okay.

> *LIZ continues cleaning. While she's turned away, CYD takes a small bottle of whiskey out of her pocket. She takes a covert swig and then puts it back. She finishes her sandwich.*

                    LIZ

All done with that sandwich stuff? I'll take the wrapper.

> *She takes the wrapper and bag to throw them in the trash. She stops.*

Why do you smell like whiskey?

CYD

... The sandwich was made of cured meats?

LIZ

Hand it over.

CYD

I don't know what you're talking about.

LIZ

Can you give me the bottle, or flask, or thimble— please?

CYD

No, I don't think so.

LIZ

Please?

CYD

You already said that.

LIZ

Come on.

CYD

Why should I?

LIZ

Because I'm asking politely. I've cleaned your apartment and all I'm asking in return is that bottle.

CYD

What are you going to do with it? Are you gonna dump it out?

LIZ

Yup.

CYD

Then you can't have it.

LIZ

Okay, then I'm not going to dump it out.

                        CYD

Now you're just lying.

                        LIZ

Yes, I am.

                        CYD

You're definitely not getting it now.

                        LIZ

I said please.

                        CYD

And I said no.

                        LIZ

I don't want to make a whole thing out of this.

                        CYD

Out of what?

                        LIZ

Like, I don't want to have, ya know … an intervention.

                        CYD

You're goddamn right you don't!

                        LIZ

You do have a problem, you know.

                        CYD

Oh, you fucking think so?! Liz you're sooooo smart! Wherever did you learn to sleuth?!

                        LIZ

Well, the first step is admitting it.

                        CYD

The first step is fuck off.

                        LIZ

Calm down. Don't be a stereotype.

                        CYD

Fuck off.

LIZ

It's my job to not fuck off. It's my job to fuck on.

CYD

You can't just tell an alcoholic person that they're an alcoholic person while they're drinking on a mattress in the middle of the floor. You're going about this all wrong. Even I know that.

LIZ

Am I?

CYD

Yeah.

LIZ

And you know better?

CYD

I've read the damn websites, which is apparently more than you've done. First of all, we're supposed to be in a neutral location. This isn't neutral. This is my apartment. Also, you're supposed to make sure I have time to respond.

LIZ

You sound responsive enough to me.

CYD

Shut up. Also, you cannot control the outcome. So, that's a big one. You're just supposed to say "I feel like you drink too much and that makes me sad because blah blah blah fucking yadda yadda ding dong whoop-de-do."

LIZ

Have you been watching *Intervention* on your phone?

CYD

That's not important. Anyway, you can't make me do anything or not do anything, so blow it out your ass.

LIZ

That's not a very nice thing to say.

CYD

Sorry— so blow it out your ass ... please.

                              LIZ

It's curious that you know all of this stuff and yet it makes no difference to you.

                              CYD

I follow The Betty Ford Center on Twitter.

                              LIZ

Why?

                              CYD

I don't know. Why's your face so dumb?

                              LIZ

Well at least you're not being childish.

                              CYD

What did you think was going to happen? You were going to read me some Brene Brown quotes and I was going to go "Ooooh I get it, cool. Instead of liquor I'll just take up Native American basket weaving. Now let's all stand in a circle and talk about why we're worthy of love."? I'm not that easy.

                              LIZ

Here's the thing: if you don't quit, Sandy's going to drop you.

                              CYD

Whatever.

                              LIZ

And I don't think she's faking. She said if I didn't come take away the booze, get you sobered up and at least kind of sensible for the show, she's going to drop you.

                              CYD

Who the fuck does she think she is?

                              LIZ

And then you won't have anyone representing you. No agent.

                              CYD

Who needs 'em?

LIZ

How are you going to book stuff? Pound that pavement out there on your own?

CYD

Is lying here until I rot an option?

LIZ

I wasn't really supposed to tell you that.

CYD

You failed.

LIZ

I guess I did, but I'm not sure how else to talk you into this.

CYD

You know, they say you can't get someone to stop doing something for anyone but themselves.

LIZ

I know. So do it for yourself.

CYD

I don't deserve any favors from me, I haven't earned them from myself.

LIZ

You're going to burn out your liver, and you can't have mine.

CYD

You could always just kill me.

LIZ

I'll leave.

CYD

Oh, come on

LIZ

I will.

CYD

Sandy's bluffing and so are you.

                              LIZ

I'll quit, Cyd. I'll march right on out of here forever.

                              CYD

Thank God, we can finally act out the end of A Doll's House together. I am such a Torvald.

                              LIZ

Jesus. I'm trying to help you.

                              CYD

You wouldn't quit. You wouldn't have anything to quit for.

                              LIZ

What kind of stupid jab is that?

                              CYD

If you didn't have my bullshit to distract you, your life would be a fucking bore. You don't have a life without me. That's not an insult, that's just reality, my friend.

                              LIZ

That's stupid. I have other people. And a boyfriend. And people.

                              CYD

Oh yeah? Where does he live— Canada?

                              LIZ

No, he lives in Brooklyn. Give me the bottle.

                              CYD

God, what would you do? Go back to temping?

                         CYD laughs.

                              LIZ

I'm not an idiot; you're being defensive to try to piss me off and get me to forget about what I'm asking you—and it's not going to work. Just hand me the bottle, and get it over with, because I'm not going to stop asking for it. I'm just going to sit here and deflect all of your questions until you're tired. It works on toddlers. You'll just give it to me when you run out of things to say. So why not speed up the process and hand it over before you say a bunch of things you don't really mean. Okay? Can we just do that instead?

CYD

No.

LIZ

Listen, I'm not doing this because I want to.

> *She sits beside CYD.*

I'm doing it because ... I know this show is important to you. You'll never admit it, but I know. This last year hasn't been ... I mean, you're not ... Jesus, what are the words I'm looking for?

CYD

I'm a washed up loser.

LIZ

Yup, that's it.

> *CYD laughs sadly, shaking her head.*

CYD

Well, at least we've got that figured out.

LIZ

I remember the first time I ever saw you.

CYD

This isn't going to be embarrassing at all.

LIZ

You had them eating out of the palm of your hand. Maybe that phrase is overused—who cares. You probably do, I guess, but that's what they were doing and so was I—except I was at home watching you on a pretty small screen.

CYD

On basic cable. While everyone else in the world was asleep— including me.

LIZ

When you're on, you're really on. But when you're like this ... well, this sucks. I don't know how else to describe it. You're still in there, I know, but it's like you're trapped or something. And I know I'm not doing this the way that anyone is supposed to do anything but I don't know what else to do but to be honest with you. And you're not the kind of person who would allow yourself to be saved, so ... now what?

CYD

Hell if I know.

LIZ

That's the best I can do as far as rousing heartfelt speeches go. I don't know what goes on in your head and I can't fix anything but I know that I don't want you to give up just yet. You're not the patron saint of drinkers. I mean … and you're not Frances Farmer either, you know? You can be okay. I believe that. May I have the bottle now?

CYD

No, you may not.

> *CYD takes the bottle out and quickly downs the rest of the liquor, then tosses the bottle on the floor.*

CYD

But I won't get another one.

LIZ

Really?

CYD

Just so I don't have to listen to anymore heartfelt speeches. That one was pretty terrible.

LIZ

Yeah, I know. You could at least have thrown the bottle in the trash.

CYD

But then what would you do?

LIZ

Shut up.

> *LIZ grabs the trash bag, picks up the bottle, and tosses it in.*

ACT I

SCENE 6

> *An open mic at a comedy club four days later— same set up as the first open mic scene. CYD stands next to a stool which contains a glass and a small pitcher of water. She looks tired, sweaty, and generally like shit. Her hands are shaky.*

CYD

I, uh … my mother called me the other day and, uh … she was … she said she was … um …

Really long pause. She fills the glass with water.

CYD

What if I filled this up all the way and then didn't drink any? Wouldn't that make you crazy? That would make me crazy, if I had to watch that. Ahhhhh shit. Sometimes I envy people with day jobs and work weeks because they're always so fucking excited about Friday. Everywhere I go it's like "Ohhh, happy Friday!" And I'm like "I don't have those. I just have a whole year of the same thing every day. Each 24 hour period is a series of events eerily similar to the previous day's events in that there are no events and it's a dark tunnel of meaningless breathing and hoping not to choke to death on a sandwich while also recognizing that if you did, that would probably not be such a big deal because whether it happens now or in 20 years, there won't be much difference, you'll still be watching VHS tapes of Murphy Brown you recorded off the TV, and probably wearing the same shirt." And they're like, "Here's your coffee, ma'am." And I'm like, "Cool, can I hang out here? What are you doing later?"

She sips the water and looks down for a moment.

Uh … I'm a little bit … uh, fucking, whatever. I mean, Jesus. Have you ever fucking … .Like, have you ever done this shit before? I mean you don't know what … christ.

She drinks more water.

Actually, I'm gonna sit on this stool. I don't know why I wasn't already doing that.

She sets the glass of water and pitcher on the floor, then sits on the stool.

When I was a kid … I wanted to be a … I thought I'd be a gymnast, probably because I have no sense of importance about my personal safety … and that's why I do this with my life.

She laughs to herself and rubs her head. She tries to reach down for the glass of water without standing up. This takes a while and doesn't go well. There is a long beat while she looks down at her knees, trying to reason with herself about how to go on. She looks around the room.

What would we call the decor in here? Hung over funeral?

She laughs at herself and shakes her head. She jumps around from topic to topic, unable to focus and getting increasingly irritable.

That's probably the name of my memoir. I wonder if I'll ever be one of those women who uses hand cream. I wonder what their lives are like. You know what really pisses me off? Breathing. I can't stand it. It's a fucking waste of time. A fucking waste of fucking time. It's a fucking, goddamn, son of a bitch, piece of shit waste of fucking time. Jesus Christ, shouldn't you be at home with your kids? Everyone's got kids and they should be at home with their fucking kids. Not me, that's why I'm here. You think if I had other shit to do I'd be in this hell hole? You think I'm having a good time at the Chuckle Shack or whatever the hell this place is called on Fridays when they have comedy instead of ukulele renditions of top 40 songs? Ukulele players— now, those are some people who should kill themselves. What— is your mother in a 12 piece ukulele band? Fuck off. FUCK OFF. What do you want, anyway? I'm not a fucking wind-up toy. But if you want me to dance, I'll fucking dance.

She stands and kicks the stool over. She drops the mic on the floor.

Do I get to be Marc Maron now? Now that I'm a fucking lunatic?! Yeah, buddy, put it on YouTube so I can watch it when I'm 40, if I live to 40. And if I don't, you can post it on fuckin' Facebook and say "Isn't this poignant now that she died at 39? Isn't this fucking meaningful?" I hope all of this is making you feel better about yourself. Good for you. Good for somebody.

Blackout.

End of Act I.

ACT 2

SCENE 1

The day of the show taping. The apartment has been cleaned up. Maybe there are finally some sheets on the bed. Everything's been straightened up. The trash is gone, there are no bottles lying around. There is now a chair in the room. Lights up on CYD sitting in the chair. She's wearing a robe. She looks better than before. She's sober. SANDY sits on the bed, looking a mixture of pleased and slightly anxious.

CYD

Sandy, keep it together. You look like you've got restless body syndrome.

SANDY

What? I always look like this!

CYD

Yeah, I know.

LIZ enters from the bathroom carrying a makeup bag. She digs through it.

LIZ

Okay, how are we feeling about lipstick?

CYD

I don't feel about lipstick.

SANDY

HA! Good one! On a roll— she's a on a roll!

LIZ

I think anything with an orangey undertone would be a nightmare with your skin.

CYD

Thank you?

LIZ

But I have this great berry colored business in here somewhere.

LIZ digs around in her makeup bag.

CYD

Let's not go crazy on this stuff, okay? I do still need to look like myself.

LIZ

Everybody looks worse on TV, so if you look, like, way better in person then you'll probably be sort of kind of presentable on screen.

SANDY

She's right. Have you ever seen Cher without makeup? Hoooo boy. But she's much older than you. I mean, you look a little uh, you know, rode hard and put away wet, but you've still got some of your youth!

CYD

You always know just what to say.

LIZ

How are you feeling?

CYD

Gassy.

SANDY

I've got some Pepto— you want some Pepto? I got Pepto!

LIZ

Please don't say that to Dan Lennon.

CYD

Guys, calm down. I'm fine, okay? Everything is going to be fine. I'm bathed, I'm conscious— and with this fashionable new lipstick, what could possibly go wrong?

She takes the lipstick from LIZ and holds it up next to her face, speaking like a commercial.

CYD

Chemical Face's new Berry Berry Quite Contrary lipstick goes on smooth and makes my mouth a foreign red color—and I like that! May cause blindness in children under 40—

To the tune of the Maybelline jingle.

Maybe it's Chemical Face!

SANDY

… You're not gonna do that on camera, are you?

CYD glares lightly at SANDY.

                              LIZ

Being beautiful is hard.

> *Handing CYD a compact mirror.*

Tell me that doesn't look pretty good.

                              CYD

I'll live.

                              LIZ

You're allergic to being impressed, aren't you?

                              SANDY

Let me see!

> *She approaches CYD to check out the makeup job.*

Say, look at you! Not bad! No, not bad at all! Well, heck. Ya look great, Cyd. You look real good.

> *LIZ takes her cell phone out of her pocket and checks it.*

                              CYD

Stop checking the time. We're fine.

                              SANDY

What's this, though? You have a little something right here.

> *SANDY tries to scratch something off of CYD's face.*

                              LIZ

I'm not. I'm expecting a call from Clark.

> *CYD is silent.*

Clark ... you know ... my boyfriend, Clark.

                              CYD

Oh yeah. No, I knew that.

                              SANDY

Man, it is REALLY stuck on there.

                              LIZ

Your memory is a real nightmare.

CYD

Sandy, that's part of my face. A freckle or something. Stop burrowing into my flesh. And yeah, my memory is terrible. Always has been. I can't remember anything before the age of 16.

SANDY

Really? Ugh. Get that checked.

LIZ

That can't be true.

CYD

No, really! I can remember sort of still images of certain places or people, but otherwise I can't really remember anything that happened—probably because nothing happened.

LIZ

You didn't fall desperately in love with some teenaged hunk?

CYD

Not really.

LIZ

I did. Pretty much every week.

CYD

Figures.

SANDY

Figures! HA!

LIZ

Yeah. Wait, how does that figure?

CYD

Because you're one of those affection people.

LIZ

What?

CYD

You need affection.

SANDY

I'm gonna have to agree with Cyd on that one.

LIZ

Says the woman preparing for a television appearance in four hours.

CYD

Yeah, but that's not affection, that's attention.

LIZ

What's the difference?

CYD

The possibility of love, I guess.

SANDY

You're not gonna say that on the show, are ya?

CYD

Not everything I say is something I'm gonna say. You're killin' me. Calm down. Have a ginger ale.

SANDY

Good idea. Do you have ginger ale?

CYD

No.

LIZ

That's the first time I've ever heard you use the word "love".

CYD

Yeah, I hated it. I need a mint.

SANDY

I'm gonna go get a ginger ale.

SANDY makes for the door.

LIZ

You're just as susceptible to love as anybody else.

CYD

Whatever you say.

LIZ

FAKE LASHES!

                              CYD

What?

         SANDY turns back to agree.

                             SANDY

Yes! Just like Cher!

         SANDY exits.

                              LIZ

You need fake lashes. But I don't have steady enough hands to put them on another person. You'll have to do it yourself; here.

         She digs a set of false lashes out of her makeup bag and hands them to CYD.

There's a little tube of glue and you just put a line of it on there and slap 'em on!

                              CYD

Why don't I think it'll be that easy?

                              LIZ

Because you're a pessimist.

                              CYD

Oh right, I forgot.

                              LIZ

You know, I think you almost had.

         LIZ exits to the bathroom. CYD applies a line of glue to a strip of lashes. She looks in the too-small mirror and tries to position it on her eyelid. She gets frustrated, then smirks and sticks them on her forehead. They look like a floating unibrow.

                              LIZ

(*off*) How's it going in there?

                              CYD

Really, really great!

                              LIZ

(*off*) Really?

CYD

Totally! I have a real knack for this!

LIZ

(off) Hooray!

CYD

I look just like Sophia Loren!

> *To herself.*

If she were also a mutant.

> *The apartment buzzer goes off. CYD pushes a button to buzz the person in. She sits down and admires her handiwork in the mirror.*

CYD

This is some Picasso shit.

> *There is a knock at the door.*

CYD

Come in with your damn ginger ale and see the art that I have made on my face!

> *SOME GUY enters and stops when he sees CYD. After a moment, she turns and sees him. She jumps out of the chair.*

CYD

What the fuck are you doing here?

SOME GUY

Uh, I-

CYD

Get the hell out of here or I'll call the police. And I hate the police.

SOME GUY

Take it easy.

CYD

Take it home.

SOME GUY

Just wait-

> *LIZ enters from the bathroom.*

LIZ

What's all the- Oh, there you are!

CYD

What the fuck is going on?

LIZ links arms with SOME GUY.

LIZ

You're going to have to forgive me.

CYD

Why? What did you do?

LIZ

I know you hate surprises, but I knew if I told you I was bringing him here to meet you-

CYD

Meet me-

LIZ

-that you'd find a reason to say no. So, here he is! Clark— Cyd, Cyd— Clark.

Beat. CYD and SOME GUY say nothing.

Ta-daaaaa!

Beat.

Oh my God!

CYD AND SOME GUY

Both terrified they've been figured out.

W-what? I, uh, whaaaat? Well, uh … no, I just …

LIZ

That is NOT where eyelashes are supposed to go.

CYD

What? Oh, I-

LIZ

Take those things off before they mess up your foundation!

CYD

Okay...

CYD slowly peels the lashes off of her face. Her eyes are glued to SOME GUY's.

CYD

So... how did you two... meet?

LIZ starts scratching at CYD's face to make sure any adhesive residue comes off.

SOME GUY

Oh... just... around.

CYD

Uh-huh.

SOME GUY

How do you two, uh, know each other?

CYD

She didn't say?

SOME GUY

No.

LIZ

I just told him I'm a personal assistant, didn't tell him to who— figured I'd surprise him with it later! You know, once I figured he was important enough to know.

CYD

And he... is important enough to know?

LIZ

Obviously. *(whispering)* Stop being a weirdo.

CYD

She's my assistant, in case you didn't make that connection just now.

SOME GUY

Ah.

LIZ

Did you recognize her?

SOME GUY

Yea-I mean … I don't-

LIZ

Don't be shy! See, Cyd, you're still famous enough for people to know you!

CYD

Hooray.

LIZ

Don't mind her, she's always like this.

SOME GUY nods.

LIZ

These lashes are screwed. I'll go downstairs and get some new ones from that weird dollar store. They'll probably give you some sort of toxic poisoning or something, but they'll have to do since you messed these up. I'll be right back. You guys can do all that fun getting-to-know-you stuff!

LIZ gives SOME GUY a quick kiss on the cheek.

Relax, she's just a person.

LIZ exits out the front door. Beat.

CYD

I really don't remember doing lots of hallucinogens this morning so what the fuck is going on here?

SANDY re-enters with a can of ginger ale. CYD and SOME GUY fall silent.

SANDY

Hey guys!

They say nothing.

SANDY

You look familiar! Who are you?

SOME GUY

Clark.

SANDY

Ohhhhh Liz's guy!

SOME GUY

Yup.

SANDY

Cool. Cool.

> *SANDY cracks open her ginger ale. She sips it loud and slow. It is the only sound in the room.*

SANDY

Okie dokie! I'm just gonna have a seat here.

> *She sits on the edge of the bed again. She sips her soda. CYD and SOME GUY absorb the silence.*

SANDY

Goooood ginger ale. Very refreshing. Made with real ginger. So says the can.

CYD

So, uh ... when are you going to tell her?

SOME GUY

I'm not sure I know what you're talking about.

SANDY

Tell who what?

CYD

I think you do.

SOME GUY

You must be thinking of somebody else.

CYD

HA!

> *She clears her throat.*

Well, this is certainly quite the ... thing.

SOME GUY

Whatever you're thinking, you might as well forget about it.

                           CYD

I don't think so. Hadn't you better run along?
                        SOME GUY

I'm right where I'm supposed to be.
                           CYD

I disagree.
                          SANDY

Are we doing a skit right now?
                           CYD

He was just leaving.
                        SOME GUY

I was just staying.
                           CYD

You can't be fucking serious. What dimension are you living in right now?!
                          SANDY

Is this a skit?
                           CYD

SKETCH, Sandy. Fucking sketch. And no, it isn't.
                          SANDY

Language! You're gonna be on TV!

CYD approaches SOME GUY, they are half-whispering.
                           CYD

You can't seriously think you two are going to continue to be... whatever you are.
                        SOME GUY

I do seriously think that, yes. We're very happy.
                           CYD

You're very happy.
                        SOME GUY

Yes.

CYD

Fascinating. Good. Wonderful. Sandy, isn't it great when two people are truly happy together?

SANDY

Awww, yeah I like that! My ex husband didn't but who needs him?! HA!

CYD

And are honest with each other and stop fucking other people?

SANDY

Uhhh, yeah!

CYD

Isn't it amazing when people aren't terrible human beings who screw everything up and don't try to, I don't know, strangle other people? Like, try to kill them and then somehow pretend like it never happened?

SANDY

Are you sure this isn't a skit?

SOME GUY

Oh God. This chick is hilarious! You have a hell of a comic here, Sandy!

SANDY

Thank you! See, Cyd, people still believe in you.

SOME GUY

How's that ginger ale, by the way?

SANDY

Really good! Thank you for asking! You know-

CYD

Well if you don't tell her, I guess I always could.

SOME GUY

She wouldn't believe you.

CYD

Oh really?

SOME GUY

So don't bother. Wouldn't turn out well for you, anyway.

CYD

Yeah, I think I will tell her myself.

SOME GUY

You know what? Go ahead. But I don't think you have any stones to throw.

> *SANDY looks at her phone. She answers it.*

SANDY

Sharon! Yeah! I saw that Letterman set the other night. Good stuff, good stuff!

> *SANDY wanders into the bathroom to talk on the phone. SOME GUY starts looking at stuff in the room— touching things, inspecting his surroundings a little. He is calm.*

SOME GUY

I didn't try to kill you. If I had tried to kill you, you'd be dead.

> *Noticing the floor.*

You know you oughtta get a Swiffer. Picks up dust pretty good.

CYD

That was a gross thing to say. The first thing, not the Swiffer thing. You're probably right about the Swiffer thing. I'm telling her, so you might as well delete her number from your phone because you're as good as gone.

SOME GUY

I don't think so.

CYD

Well I do. And I love being right.

SOME GUY

I mean … personally, if my friend picked up my significant other at a bar and took them home, I don't know if I'd be so forgiving about it. But maybe that's just me. Especially when my friend is a well-known liar with a pretty intense drinking problem.

CYD

Hey, I quit. And I didn't know you were her boyfriend, fucking obviously.

SOME GUY

That's weird, I distinctly remember telling you that I had a girlfriend named Elizabeth Daniels who has blonde hair and a warm smile.

CYD

No you didn't. You know you didn't.

SOME GUY

And you said "That's weird, that's my assistant's name!" And through a series of delightful anecdotes, we figured out it was the same person. Wasn't that so funny?

CYD

That is hilariously stupid.

SOME GUY

I guess we'll just have to see if she agrees with you.

CYD

You think she would even consider keeping you around when she hears about this?

SOME GUY shrugs.

SOME GUY

I don't know, but I know she wouldn't keep you around. I mean, if you had a choice, would you keep you around?

CYD

What the hell do you expect me to do?

SOME GUY

Nothing. You don't have to worry about her. She's fine. We're fine.

CYD

Get out of here.

SOME GUY

And how would you explain that to Elizabeth?

CYD

Stop calling her Elizabeth! Nobody calls her Elizabeth!

SOME GUY

I call her Elizabeth.

LIZ enters through the front door. SANDY re-enters from the bathroom.

LIZ

Got 'em! Sit down. I guess I'll have to do my best to put them on for you, since you're clearly unstable. I hope they don't melt your eyelids off or anything. Who knows what the hell this adhesive is made of!

CYD hesitates for a second, then sits down on the chair.

SANDY

That was Sharon Esposito on the phone. You know she was just on Letterman?

CYD gives her a death stare.

SOME GUY

Could I use the bathroom?

LIZ

Pointing.

Yup, it's right over there!

SOME GUY exits to the bathroom.

CYD

Ya know, it's my bathroom.

LIZ

What, you weren't going to let him use the bathroom?

CYD

I don't know, I didn't get a chance to answer him. It's in the realm of possibility that I might just let him piss in the corner instead.

LIZ

Excited.

Well, what do you think?

CYD

Liz-

LIZ

Oh come on! Give him a chance!

CYD

What do you like about this guy?

LIZ

Well, he's good looking, obviously.

CYD

So was Hitler.

LIZ

No, he wasn't.

CYD

No, he wasn't. That was a test. If you had said Hitler was attractive I'd have to discount your opinion.

SANDY

They're totally different, Clark doesn't even have a mustache.

LIZ

Oh God.

CYD

What else do you like about him?

LIZ

He's polite.

CYD

Since when is that at the top of the list when you're looking for … whatever he's supposed to be?

LIZ

I didn't say it was at the top! I'm just … listing stuff. It's not in any particular order. Uh, he's nice to me!

CYD

Really?

LIZ

Is that so hard to believe?

CYD

What else? Concrete things!

LIZ

I don't know! What's a concrete thing when it comes to love?

CYD

LOVE?

LIZ

Now you've said it twice! Haha!

CYD

What ELSE? Come on, Liz. Something real.

LIZ

I don't know, okay? I just know that I like him. I really like him. Like, a lot. And I want you to like him. I want him to stick around.

SANDY

Awwwww!

LIZ AND CYD

Shut up, Sandy!

> SANDY sips her ginger ale and watches the following.

CYD

What if I don't like him?

LIZ

You don't even know him.

CYD

Right, what if I get to know him and I don't like him?

SANDY

I like him!

LIZ

So, you don't like him.

CYD

Would you keep seeing him anyway?

LIZ

Uh, I don't-

CYD

Would you?

LIZ

God, I don't know! You're not letting me think.

CYD

There shouldn't be anything to think about.

LIZ

Why are you making such a big deal out of this?

CYD

If I take the time to assess this suitor, and find him unsuitable, if I fucking hate his guts, if I think he's a bad person— are you still going to see him?

Beat. LIZ says nothing.

CYD

Well, are you?!

LIZ

Yes! Okay? Yes. If you don't like him, that's not going to make me not like him. Can't you ever just say yes to anything?

CYD

What if I think he's the devil?

LIZ

Okay, what?

CYD

What if I think he's Lucifer himself?

SANDY

Cyd, take it easy! You're gonna get bulging veins in your forehead!

CYD

I'M FINE.

LIZ

Have you been reading those pamphlets in the mail? Why are you being so crazy? Stop fucking with me. You have to finish getting ready.

CYD

I'm not fucking with you, Liz. If I said that ... that ...

LIZ

CLARK! His name is Clark.

CYD

If I said that Clark ate a baby, would you stop seeing him?

LIZ

Do you have proof that he ate a baby, in this completely absurd, hypothetical, ridiculous situation?

CYD

No. But I know that he did. I can't give you evidence, but I know that he did and I swear to it and you just have to believe me. You just have to go on my word and my word alone. Would you stop seeing him?

SOME GUY enters from the bathroom.

SOME GUY

Beautiful accommodations in there.

CYD

... What?

SOME GUY

The bathroom. I'm just saying— nice bathroom.

CYD

Nice bathroom?

LIZ

He's just being polite. Don't be weird.

CYD

Grumbling to herself.

Polite. Nice. Great, what's next— genial? Amiable? Clark, it seems you're just ducky! My goodness, you're all the good boring words in the dictionary

LIZ

Clark's going to come watch the show with me, isn't that cool?

CYD

What do you mean? In the audience?

LIZ

Of course.

CYD

He can't do that.

To SOME GUY.

You can't do that!

SOME GUY

Uh.

LIZ

Firmly.

Well that's what he's doing.

CYD

It's not like he gives a shit— right? What did you tell him, that he was going to some random basic cable taping? It's not like he was going because I was gonna be there. So what does he care if he doesn't go?

SOME GUY

I love Dan Lennon!

CYD

Great. Stay home.

SOME GUY

Liz asked me to, and I said yes, that's all. I hear you're still pretty funny, by the way.

CYD

Yeah, not anymore. *(beat)* You can't go if you don't have a seat. You have to tell them in advance, ya know. You can't just show up.

LIZ

I had Sandy ask for an extra ticket a month ago.

CYD

A month ago? You didn't say anything! God damn it, Sandy!

SANDY

I was just bein' nice!

LIZ

I didn't think it made any difference to you who was in the audience. You're performing for strangers, after all. And I guess I thought you'd want me to be, I don't know, happy.

CYD

Yeah, but-

LIZ

Please? I mean, he's already here and everything.

SOME GUY

Hey, hey. Don't worry, Elizabeth. I want Cyd to be comfortable. I don't have to go.

SANDY

Awwww!

CYD

Ughhhhhh!

LIZ

No, Clark, I think you should come. I want you to come and sit with me.

SOME GUY

I'll leave it up to Cyd. What do you think, Cyd?

> *He casually puts his arm around LIZ's shoulders. CYD looks like she wants to carve him up like a turkey and serve him to some pilgrims.*

CYD

I think I gotta take a piss. Or did you get him a seat to that too?

> *She exits to the bathroom, angrily.*

LIZ

I'm sorry. She's ... well, you don't know her, but-

SOME GUY

I think I do.

LIZ

She's going through some stuff right now and she's just a little ... edgy, you know? Actually the edgy part is normal. She's just sort of moody ... actually that's pretty standard, too. I'm not sure what to say. She's just not herself, but she is. I should have waited longer to introduce you ... or maybe I should have done it earlier. I don't know. She's probably just nervous about the show.

SOME GUY

I don't think that girl has ever been nervous in her life.

SANDY

I wish she'd get nervous once in a while.

SOME GUY

You know what I think?

LIZ

What?

SOME GUY

She's jealous. Doesn't want you to be snatched up by some stranger. Christ, look around— What else does she have? Of course she doesn't want to lose you. I wouldn't either. I don't.

He smirks. She smiles. He kisses her, gently.

SOME GUY

She doesn't have to like me, you know. It doesn't matter. All that matters is that you like me.

LIZ

Yeah, I guess you're okay.

SOME GUY

Am I? Gee, thanks!

They laugh together.

SANDY

Awwwww!

LIZ

She's just— I mean, she's important to me. I want you to know that.

SOME GUY

I hear ya.

LIZ

We've done a lot for each other, you know.

SOME GUY

Kind of seems like you're the one doing all the doing, but I'm not gonna tell you what to do.

LIZ

You just met her today, so it's not— I mean, you can never understand another person's relationship to someone else, you know? No one can get that. Not unless they're in it too. And even then, you've only got your side.

SOME GUY

Sure.

LIZ

If those things could be explained to someone else, we wouldn't have Romeo and Juliet.

SOME GUY

Romeo and Juliet aren't real.

LIZ

You know what I mean.

SOME GUY

I'm just sayin', from where I'm standing, right here? Only one of you is leaning on the other.

LIZ

I don't think that's-

SOME GUY

Hey, hey don't worry about it. I'm not saying anything. She's your friend for whatever reason, I know that. I also know how I feel about you and I just want you to be happy. Is that okay?

LIZ

I can live with that.

She smiles. He kisses her again, his hand on her neck, mirroring his choking of CYD— but he's not choking her. CYD enters and seeing them kissing, immediately notices him touching her neck.

CYD

HEY!

LIZ

Startled.

God, I know you're edgy but you don't have to yell.

CYD

Realizing he wasn't harming her.

Oh ... I'm not fucking edgy, Liz.

SANDY

We should get going!

CYD

Go ahead.

LIZ

All of us, Cyd. They'll have to check your hair and makeup.

CYD

We just did my hair and makeup, if they were going to do it why'd we do it?

LIZ

It's basic cable, who knows what they'd do to your face if they were starting from scratch.

CYD

God damn it.

LIZ

There. That's your last swear until the show's over. Are you ready?

CYD

Close enough.

They put their coats on and LIZ grabs a couple of garment bags and things to take with them. SOME GUY is waiting in the doorway for the other two, who are on the opposite side of the room. LIZ holds one of the bags out to CYD.

SANDY

This is gonna be great!

SANDY exits.

LIZ

Here.

CYD

I thought you were going to carry them.

LIZ

You take one and I'll take one.

CYD

Fine.

LIZ

And that question you asked me before, about the baby eater?

CYD

Yeah?

LIZ

The answer is "no".

LIZ meets SOME GUY at the front door. They exit together. CYD stands silent a moment. She looks down at the bag. She is about to leave, when she spots LIZ's cell phone sitting on the chair (or a table). She picks it up.

CYD

Liz, you forgot your-

She thinks better of it, takes out her little notebook and pen, enters the pass code on the phone, and writes something down. She puts her notebook away and exits after them.

ACT II

SCENE 2

Later that night, hours after the show. CYD is sitting on the edge of her bed, lost in thought. She peels the fake eyelashes off of her eyelids. She takes off her shoes. She wipes her lipstick off on her arm. She exits to the bathroom to change clothes. After a moment, there is a knock on the door.

CYD

(*off*) Just a sec!

The pounding gets louder and more frequent. CYD comes out of the bathroom wearing her version of pajamas. They are decidedly un-glamorous: a worn out tank top or a long T-shirt and no pants. She walks slowly to the door and opens it. SANDY is standing in the doorway holding flowers and a gift basket.

SANDY

That Sean Connery bit— GOLD! I wouldn't have thought it; it didn't seem like anything to write home about when you mentioned it to me at least a dozen times in the last year, but boy— that was somethin'!

CYD

Yeah, you mentioned that.

SANDY

That couldn't have gone any better if I'd dreamed it!

CYD

Get better dreams.

SANDY

And that bit about— what was it? Something about-

CYD

Yeah, thanks.

SANDY

Yeah, that one! I gotta tell ya, Cyd, I think this is just what you needed. A nice, solid victory. Really, a great night. Just so great! Didn't you think it was great?

CYD

Sure.

SANDY

Aren't you going to invite me to sit down? Say, why didn't you hang around to celebrate after? I wanted to take you out for uh … frozen yogurt or something! Whatever you like, you must like something.

CYD straightens out the comforter and gestures for SANDY to sit

on the bed. She sits, and CYD sits next to her. They sit in silence for a moment, SANDY nodding happily, the nods eventually fading away.

SANDY

So, let's talk about the next step.

CYD

What step?

SANDY

This was great stuff, but if you wanna stay on that upward trajectory we have to operate this thing like a machine— get you booked up every night of the week! Playin' at some respectable small clubs, then keep working your way back up the ladder!

CYD

Back up?

SANDY

You know, back to where ya used to be— and farther than that even!

CYD

Uh-huh.

SANDY

How long until you have a solid 45? A month? That seems like long enough to get 45 minutes. Let's say a month.

CYD

Okay.

SANDY

Oh yeah, Dan Lennon got ya a gift basket! His people did, anyway. I doubt he called 1-800-FLOWERS himself or anything ya know, but it's the thought that counts.

She looks at the flowers.

What do they call these, daisies?

CYD

I have no idea.

SANDY

Yeah, I guess you wouldn't.

CYD looks at SANDY with light disdain.

CYD

Yeah.

SANDY

Suddenly noticing her demeanor.

Hey, kid, that's a pretty long face for someone who isn't wearing pants.

CYD shrugs.

SANDY

Wanna tell your old pal Sandy about it?

CYD

Do you like him?

SANDY

Sure, Dan's a great host and he gives gift baskets! Cute little rump on him, too, if ya like 'em skinny.

CYD

Not him. That guy Liz is dating.

SANDY

Oh, Clark?

CYD

Something like that.

SANDY

He seems okay, I guess. I mean, I'm not takin' him home to meet the parents or anything but he seems like an okay guy. And Liz really likes him. He's a blue collar kinda guy, I like blue collar kinda guys.

CYD

Why do you say she really likes him?

SANDY

I have eyes, don't I? I can see.

CYD

Sure.

SANDY

I see what I see.

CYD

Okay.

SANDY

Why, what about him?

CYD

I don't know. I don't trust him.

SANDY

Why not?

CYD

I just don't. He doesn't look like a trustworthy person.

SANDY

Okay, so don't give him the pin number for your debit card.

CYD

I don't have a debit card.

SANDY

I know, but if ya had one, you shouldn't give him the pin number.

CYD

What about Liz?

SANDY

Liz? Liz can take care of herself.

CYD

I'm not so sure about that.

SANDY

I'm pretty sure of it.

CYD

Well, I'm not, okay? So what do I do?

SANDY

I think you should just let it play out.

CYD

Getting progressively testier.

Play out?

SANDY

Don't interfere and just see what happens.

CYD

What if what happens is that she gets hurt?

SANDY

That's life.

CYD

Forget it. Forget I said anything and get the fuck out of here. God damn it, you drive me crazy. You're like all those guys who are really into coke, you know? God damn it, you're annoying.

SANDY

Hey— whoa— I do not do blow!

CYD

People who don't do blow, don't call it blow.

SANDY

And I don't deserve that kinda talk! You asked me what I thought you should do, and I gave you my opinion! Meddling ain't a great thing for friendship; that's all I'm sayin'. Ya gotta give people their space.

CYD

So give me some right now.

SANDY

See— this is what I'm talkin' about. You go ahead and tell her what to do and see how well that goes. It worked pretty good just now when I did it to you, didn't it? *(beat)* I'll call ya in a few days. Work on gettin' up to 45 minutes. Enjoy your gift basket.

SANDY exits. CYD starts looking through the gift basket.

CYD

Laughing to herself.

45 minutes. What the fuck does she know about 45 minutes.

She finds various fancy snacks and/or knick knacks with the show logo on them. Then she spots something in the bottom of the basket and pulls it out. It's a large bottle of expensive bourbon with a ribbon tied around it. She sets it down next to her and opens a bag of M&Ms from the basket. She eats them while looking at the bottle. She lies down in bed and looks at the bottle, still snacking on candies, the bottle close to her face. Lights slowly fade out as she falls asleep.

ACT II

SCENE 3

Two hours later. Lights half up. CYD is asleep, still holding the bag of M&Ms. There is rapid knocking at the door. CYD is startled. She gets up quickly and grabs something she could possibly use as a weapon. She opens the door, expecting something potentially bad. DEB stands in the doorway.

DEB

SURPRIIIIIISE!

CYD is silent.

Let me in, already! I ain't got all day!

CYD

It's night.

DEB

Well I ain't got all night, either!

CYD

How did you get past the buzzer?

DEB

Aw, I just picked the lock.

CYD

Great. Good. Tight security here. Everybody gets in. It's really late. It's way, way too late. Why aren't you home? Go home.

DEB

Your home is my home!

                             CYD

It really isn't.

>   *DEB sits down on the bed.*

                             DEB

Sit yourself right now here next to me!

                             CYD

I don't feel like it.

                             DEB

Come on, now!

                             CYD

I'm not-

                             DEB

There's a nice spot right here for ya!

                             CYD

I know— it's my bed.

                             DEB

So sit on it!

                             CYD

Mom, I'm fucking busy, okay?

                             DEB

Doin' what?

                             CYD

Sleeping. It's this thing I'm trying. So, just … please go. I'm very tired.

                             DEB

Hell's bells, Cyd, I'm not movin' in. I just had the sudden desire to talk to my darling daughter and that's just what I'm goin' to do. Park it.

>   *She pats the bed again.*

Ya ain't gettin' rid of me, so you might as well sit down.

>   *CYD sits next to her, reluctantly.*

So, what's new?

CYD

Nothing. Everything's exactly the same as it always is.

DEB

Some people go their whole damn lives lookin' for that kinda consistency!

CYD

Probably not this kind.

DEB

No? Ah, well. Doesn't matter ... aren't ya gonna ask what's new with me?

CYD

I didn't really intend to, no.

DEB

All kinds of shit is new with me! I got a job now, I got a pretty good boyfriend-

CYD

You got a job? Somebody hired you?

DEB

(cackling) You're damn right they did! Did you hear the part where I have a new boyfriend?

CYD

Yeah, I did.

DEB

Well, aren't you gonna ask me about him?

CYD

No, I'm not. Can I go to sleep now?

DEB

No, you can't. His name's Jake— isn't that great? Sounds like the name of a guy who rides a motorcycle, doesn't it?

CYD

Does he ride a motorcycle?

DEB

No, but he could!

CYD

I bet.

DEB

This place looks nice than I remember. You get a maid or somethin'?

CYD

Nope.

DEB

Sure looks like someone's takin' care of it.

CYD

I could be taking care of it myself, you know.

DEB

(cackling) That's a good one! You haven't cleaned anything up since that time you dropped my cold cream on the floor and I whooped your behind! Boy, you sure did get to cleaning then!

CYD

I was 7. Do we really need to talk about that shit anymore?

DEB

Hey! Honor thy father and mother and all that. Don't swear at me. I got rights.

CYD

Are you drunk?

DEB

Yeah, aren't you?

CYD

I quit.

DEB

Quit?! Since when?

CYD

A few weeks ago.

DEB

Then what's that bottle of bourbon doing over there?

CYD

It was a gift from some people who didn't know better.

DEB

Maybe they knew better than you think.

DEB grabs the bottle.

CYD

Ma, leave that alone. I don't want that open right now.

CYD takes out her e-cigarette and puffs away on it, dissatisfied with what it supplies.

DEB

What do you care? Someone oughtta drink it! I think I'm just what it needs.

She opens the bottle. CYD looks a little nervous. DEB takes a pull from the bottle.

Hoooooo boy! That's the ticket! Say, what's this basket about?

CYD

It's a gift basket. The bourbon came with it.

DEB

Is this because of that TV thing? Jake's son told me you were gonna be on TV. He keeps up with all that internet news shit at the library. Can't get the little bastard to read a book, though. Figures.

CYD

It was taped today. They'll play it in a few days.

DEB

I'll have Jake set the TiVo. When we get a TiVo!

She laughs at her own joke. CYD does not.

Say, what crawled up your ass, anyway?

CYD

I told you, ma. I'm tired.

DEB

Don't you think I'm tired? I mentioned I have a new job, right?

CYD

Yes. Is your memory going?

DEB

I just want to make sure I mentioned it, is all.

DEB takes another pull from the bottle.

So, you must be doing better now, huh?

CYD

I'm pretty tired of people making it sound like I wasn't doing well before.

DEB

Well, you know what I mean.

CYD

Sure.

DEB

I just wanted to see how you were doing. You are my baby girl, after all.

DEB puts her arm around CYD's shoulder.

Listen, I know I haven't always been June Beaver or anything, but I'm still your mother.

CYD

Cleaver.

DEB

What?

CYD

Cleaver. June Cleaver. Beaver is the kid's name.

DEB

Yeah that's what I said. The point is, I'm still your mother.

CYD

I haven't forgotten.

DEB

Good. That's good. That's a good thing to remember.

There is a longish pause. DEB's arm remains around CYD's shoulder. CYD looks conflicted.

Got any boyfriends or anything?

CYD

No, ma, I don't.

DEB

Girlfriends?

CYD gives DEB a look.

I just hope you're not all by your lonesome all the time! I did that for a while, ya know, and then I made some not-so-great choices, but who's counting? Apart from the cops, I mean … out of loneliness, probably. So now I surround myself with people and I'm great!

DEB drinks more booze.

How's that girl that's always here? What's her name … Chloe?

CYD

Her name's Liz. She's okay.

DEB

Well …

Searching her brain for something to talk about.

Well, shit, Cyd!

CYD

What?

DEB

I can't get you to tell me nothin'!

CYD

Maybe there isn't anything to tell.

DEB

'Course there is! Uh … looks like you got a new chair in here!

CYD

Yup.

DEB

Aren't you gonna tell me about it?

                                CYD

It's a fuckin' chair, ma.

                                DEB

There has to be something you can tell me about! What's new? There has to be somethin' new!

                                CYD

No.

                                DEB

C'moooon! Let your old ma inside that brain of yours! I'm just here to listen!

                                CYD

   Explosive.

Fine! You want to know what's really going on? I fucked some stupid heckler and he turned out to be Liz's boyfriend and he's crazy and violent and weird which is fine if he's crazy and violent and weird to me, because I probably fucking deserve it anyway, but I'm afraid that he's going to be that way to her and I wouldn't be able to live with myself if that happened. I can't stop thinking about drinking but if I do I know I won't be able to stop myself and I'll probably end up in a pile of trash somewhere which would honestly not even be fair to the pile of trash. The worst thing is that I know if I tell Liz that her stupid boyfriend is a piece of shit she won't even believe me and she'll just stay with him anyway, so the whole thing would be pointless— So what the fuck am I supposed to do, ma? There you go, there's your news. Now impart your motherly advice and fix everything so you can feel like you've done your job this year.

   She throws down her e-cigarette.

And I fucking hate this thing! I hate it! Fucking space ship cigarettes!

                                DEB

Jesus, Cyd.

                                CYD

Yeah, Jesus.

                                DEB

I don't know.

CYD

What a spectacular waste of time.

DEB

Sounds like you need a drink.

CYD

Are you kidding? Did you hear any of that?

DEB

I am kidding.

CYD

No, you're not. You really do think that's the solution. You've spent your whole life drumming up problems for yourself because they didn't seem to be happening quickly enough for you on their own. And now all you know how to do is make things worse.

DEB

Her daughter's intensity seems to have sobered her up a little.

You're being a little hard on your old ma, don't you think?

CYD

No, I don't think. You know why?

DEB

No ... why?

CYD

Because I know you want something.

DEB

I don't know what you're talking about.

CYD

I know that you're just here because you want something. I haven't seen you in eight months, and the last time you left really quickly when you realized my career wasn't exactly up there with the constellations.

DEB

That's not-

CYD

So how much is it?! How much do you want?

DEB

I wasn't going to-

CYD

I'm not a fucking child. Stop trying to manipulate me, just say it out loud and I'll give it to you because that's what our relationship is. That's what it's always been. C'est la fucking vie.

DEB

… Two hundred dollars.

CYD

Great.

> *CYD digs around in the pockets of her jeans and finds some wadded up bills. She tosses it at/to DEB.*

CYD

Here.

DEB

I did really get a job, so I can-

CYD

Stop. Don't offer something you can't offer.

DEB

I'd feel better if I did.

CYD

Yes, lies often feel better, don't they?

DEB

Yeah.

CYD

And don't bother telling me what it's for. I know what it's for, and I don't want to think about it. Just … don't die.

DEB

Yeah, you too.

> *CYD goes to the door and opens it, waiting for DEB to leave.*

DEB

I am still your mother, you know.

CYD

Yeah, you mentioned that.

> *DEB exits. CYD sits on the bed for a moment, clearly frustrated and conflicted. The opened bottle of bourbon sits next to her. She eventually realizes it's there and picks it up. She examines the bottle. She puts it up to her nose and smells it. As she is about to take a drink, she sets it down again and stands up. She starts walking around the room. She stops and goes through the basket again, taking out some other snack and taking a few bites before throwing it on the floor. She picks up the bottle, hesitates, and then takes a big drink. She immediately puts the bottle back on the floor. She stares at it. Disgusted with herself, she grabs a jacket, puts it on and exits.*

ACT II

SCENE 4

> *Several hours later. It is early afternoon. Lights up on LIZ sitting on the bed. CYD enters, finally coming home. She is startled by LIZ's presence in her apartment.*

CYD

What are you doing here?

LIZ

> *Holding up the bottle.*

What is this?

CYD

That is bourbon.

LIZ

Why is it here?

CYD

It came in a gift basket from Dan Lennon. Or from his people, or something.

LIZ

Why is it open?

CYD

I didn't open it.

LIZ

Then why is it open?

CYD

My ... mom opened it.

LIZ

Try again.

CYD

What?

LIZ

Your mother hasn't been here in ages. Why is this open?

CYD

Yeah, she hadn't been here in ages until she showed up in the middle of the night. Last night.

LIZ

You didn't drink any of this?

CYD

Not really.

LIZ

Not really? So you did?

CYD

What is this, a fucking investigation?

LIZ

Did you drink it or didn't you?

CYD

Not as much as it looks like I did.

CYD lights up a cigarette and starts smoking.

LIZ

I see. What happened— did you spill it?

CYD

No. My mom drank it.

LIZ

And then you had a little.

CYD

Yes. But I didn't get drunk. I just had one drink of it.

LIZ

And then-

CYD

And then I left.

LIZ

Where did you go?

CYD

Jesus, I went for a walk, Marlowe.

LIZ

I've been here three hours.

CYD

I went for a long walk.

LIZ

Did this long walk include a trip to a bar?

CYD

NO. I didn't really drink any more. I mostly just walked around.

LIZ

Why?

CYD

Because I couldn't stand to be in here anymore. Can we drop it now? What did you really come here for?

LIZ

All right. I guess I can buy that. I came here to congratulate you.

She stands up.

You were great last night.

Beat.

Congratulations.

CYD

Was I?

LIZ

You know you were.

CYD

I didn't think you'd notice.

LIZ

I was there, you know.

CYD

Yeah, well. In body, maybe.

LIZ

What's that supposed to mean?

CYD

Nothing.

LIZ

Sure. Anyway, I just wanted to say that I'm really proud of you.

CYD

Aw, shucks.

LIZ

You're welcome. For what it's worth, Clark thought you were great too.

CYD

It is, in fact, worth nothing.

LIZ

That's exactly why it is worth something. You obviously haven't been very nice to him and you certainly haven't given him a reason to like you, and he still thought you were funny. That should mean something.

CYD

No, he said he thought I was funny. That's not the same.

                           LIZ

There is literally no reason for him to lie about that.

                           CYD

He wants you to think he's a nice guy.

                           LIZ

He is a nice guy.

                           CYD

See, it's working.

                           LIZ

He is. It's not a trick. Not everyone is out to deceive you. Some people are just nice.

                           CYD

Mm-hmm.

                           LIZ

You better get used to him. He's going to be around for a while.

                           CYD

Your bullshit optimism is showing.

                           LIZ

We're talking about moving in together.

                           CYD

… No.

                           LIZ

No? I'm not asking for permission, Cyd.

                           CYD

Listen, just don't do it.

                           LIZ

I'm gonna do whatever I want. I don't understand why you can't just be happy for me. I just don't get it.

                           CYD

The two of us— we've seen some shit together.

LIZ

I've seen your shit, anyway.

CYD

I wouldn't lie to you, Liz.

LIZ

You lie to me all the time.

CYD

Not about this. He isn't good for you. He's no good in general, and in specific he is no good for you.

LIZ

How do you think you know that?

CYD

I just do.

LIZ

Did you put your hand on his forehead and read his thoughts? Did you have him secretly psychologically evaluated? Did you do a crazy background check, or a blood test? Did you take urine samples from when he peed in your toilet?

CYD

Obviously not.

LIZ

You don't know shit, Cyd. Don't you think I'd be able to tell if he were somehow the offspring of Satan? Don't you think I'm smart enough for that?

CYD

No, I don't.

LIZ

I'm not an-

They both start raising their voices.

CYD

You're a bad judge of character.

                           LIZ

Fuck that. Fuck you.

                           CYD

He's not good enough for you!

                           LIZ

Neither are you!

                           CYD

Don't you think I know that?!

> *This silences them both for a moment.*

                           LIZ

Look— I'm sorry you don't like him … I don't know what else to say.

                           CYD

And what if I say it's him or me?

                           LIZ

Don't say that and you don't have to find out.

> *LIZ moves to exit. CYD follows her.*

                           CYD

You don't know what you're doing!

                           LIZ

I swear to God, Cyd, if I find another bottle in here …

> *LIZ exits. CYD stands silent for a moment, then picks something up and throws it at the wall.*

                           CYD

Well, that wasn't as fulfilling as I thought it would be.

> *She sits in the lone chair, thinking. Then pulls out her cell phone and makes a call.*

Hey, it's Cyd. Listen, I need you to do me a favor.

ACT II

SCENE 5

Two hours later. Lights up on CYD. She stands holding the type of tall brown paper bag which always contains booze. She carefully sets it on a small table. She sets two short glasses next to it. She removes her jacket. There is a knock at the door. She opens it. DEB stands in the doorway, with a purse over her shoulder.

CYD

Come on, hurry up.

She pulls DEB into the room and closes the door.

All right, out with it.

DEB takes a small bag out of her purse.

DEB

I don't really wanna give you this without knowing what you're gonna do with it.

CYD

Just give it over.

She takes the bag and looks in it.

Is this enough? This isn't very much.

DEB

Enough for what? What are you doin'? Hey, listen, I thought I was the kooky one. You don't want to eclipse your old ma, do ya?

CYD

This is gonna have to work. All right, now go.

DEB

That's it?

CYD

That's it.

DEB

What about, uh ... ya know, I took a pretty sizable risk gettin' that shit-

CYD

You've gotten all out of me that you're gonna get. Now go away. I don't have time for … anything.

DEB

I had to spend some of that money ya gave me before on this stuff, ya know.

CYD

That's all you're getting. Drop it. You really have to go. Like, now.

CYD grabs DEB's arm and takes her to the door.

DEB

Wait, wait! I don't know what kinda shit you've gotten yourself into, but … I don't know … just don't do something stupid, okay?

CYD

Yeah, sure.

DEB

I know I never did right by you. You don't know how shitty I feel about it.

CYD

You feel fine, you're just drunk.

DEB

Getting emotional.

I'm not fucking drunk, okay? Just listen to me for a goddamn second!

CYD

Fuck.

DEB

I messed up, all right? I know that. I can't do anything about it now. You wouldn't even let me if I tried.

CYD

Stop being dramatic.

DEB

Well ya wouldn't, would ya?

CYD

No, I wouldn't.

                              DEB

        Starting to cry.

Whatever happened to second chances, huh?

                              CYD

You had about nine of them, that's what happened.

                              DEB

Whatever this is, don't do it! I can tell something's not right. I'm your mother, God damn it! You don't have to love me, just don't ruin your whole life!

                              CYD

You mean like you did?

                              DEB

Yeah, like I did.

                              CYD

Okay, you've had your time. I really can't do this right now. Stop crying like you're in a telenovela and get home. Your motorcycle boyfriend is probably waiting for you.

                              DEB

        Still crying.

He doesn't ride a motorcycle he just looks like he could.

                              CYD

I know. Good bye, ma.

                              DEB

I love you, Cyd.

                              CYD

All right.

              CYD manages to push DEB far enough through the door that she can close it. She leans against it and breathes deeply for a moment. Then she goes back to the table and takes a tiny plastic packet out of the paper bag and looks at it. There are a few small tablets inside. She places the packet on the table and proceeds to crush the tablets inside with the bottom of the liquor bottle until they are sufficiently powdery. She rummages around and finds the closest thing she has to sexy— a low cut t-shirt. She changes into it, then frantically fluffs her hair and puts on some lipstick. As she does this, she mutters to herself.

CYD

What am I doing? What am I doing? ... I'm doing what I have to. Am I? I am.

There is a knock at the door.

CYD

Oh Jesus. Okay. Come in!

SOME GUY walks in. CYD tries to look casual. They are silent.

SOME GUY

... Well?

CYD

Hm?

SOME GUY

What am I doing here?

CYD

Oh.

SOME GUY

You said I needed to come right away. What do you want?

CYD

Don't get mad at me already, it's nothing bad.

SOME GUY

Okay.

CYD

I just want to talk. Have a seat.

SOME GUY

Fine.

He sits on the bed.

Hm. Deja fuckin' vu.

CYD

Ha. Yeah. So ... oh! Care for a drink?

SOME GUY

Sure, I guess.

CYD

Pouring some liquor into the glasses.

Why don't ya take your coat off, stay a while?

SOME GUY

Uh, okay.

As he removes his jacket, she pours the crushed pills into one of the glasses and stirs it with her finger. She hands him the glass with the crushed pills in it and keeps the other glass. She sits next to him.

CYD

Here ya go. Thanks for coming over.

SOME GUY

So what do you want?

CYD

I just want to talk-

SOME GUY

About?

CYD

Liz.

SOME GUY

You look different.

He takes a sip of his drink, continuing to drink it throughout the scene.

CYD

Do I? I don't know.

SOME GUY

Yeah. You clean up okay, I guess.

CYD

Thanks. I don't want us to ... I mean ... I think it would be good if we got along, don't you?

SOME GUY

That would make things easier, yes.

CYD

Good. I don't want Liz to be unhappy or to get hurt.

SOME GUY

Neither do I.

CYD

Great. That's all I care about.

SOME GUY

Ya know, if you dressed like this more often you might even snag yourself a boyfriend.

CYD

Yeah, maybe.

SOME GUY

If you could just keep your damn mouth shut, you might be an okay girl.

He laughs and takes a drink.

CYD

I'll think about that.

SOME GUY

I'm not an asshole all the time, you know.

CYD

That's something.

SOME GUY

I get angry just like anybody.

CYD

Who doesn't?

SOME GUY

So obviously I'm not just a dick for no reason.

CYD

Who said you were?

SOME GUY

Ya know, I have to get angry. People don't just freak out. I think it's easy to forget that.

CYD

Sure.

SOME GUY

So if somebody pisses me off, I sorta feel like ... there's consequences, ya know. Like immediate karma. Like personal, immediate karma. Ya know, so if something happens it's kind of their fault too.

CYD

If what happens?

SOME GUY

Anything. You know what I mean. If anyone knows what I mean, it's you.

CYD

Me?

SOME GUY

Oh, come on. You're total chaos.

CYD

Am I?

SOME GUY

You make me look like fuckin' Mother Theresa. You're anarchy with tits. You think I'm dangerous to Liz? Come on. I mean, really, come on. I couldn't be more dangerous than you if I tried.

CYD

Maybe so.

SOME GUY

You do look different.

CYD

Yeah, I know.

SOME GUY

Come here.

CYD

Okay.

They kiss. CYD pulls back.

CYD

I'm not done with my drink yet. Let's sit here and talk for a minute and finish our drinks.

SOME GUY

Fine.

CYD

Liz told me you're talking about moving in together.

SOME GUY

Did she?

CYD

Are you?

SOME GUY

I guess so. Don't have any reason not to.

CYD

Fair enough.

SOME GUY finished his drink. CYD has barely touched hers and has mostly just been holding it. He throws back the rest of his drink.

SOME GUY

I'm done with mine. You're slow.

CYD

Yeah.

SOME GUY

You are different tonight, aren't you?

CYD

Not really.

She kisses him aggressively as the lights fade out to show the passage of time. When they come back up, SOME GUY is lying passed out on the bed, fully clothed. CYD kneels by his feet and first takes off his shoes, then his socks, and then with some difficulty— his pants. She tosses them on the floor at the end of the bed. She messes up his hair. She then applies a lot of red lipstick and carefully kisses a variety of places on his body, leaving red marks. She changes into the same 'pajamas' as before and carefully crawls into bed and waits. There is a knock at the door ... she doesn't get up to answer it. The knocking continues for a while, then a key is heard rattling in the lock. CYD whispers to herself as LIZ enters.

CYD

Oh God.

LIZ

Cyd, wake up. If you're going to ask me to come over at a specific time, you could at least be awake and maybe even answer the door. You know, if the feeling strikes you. Who did you bring home—

She realizes who it is.

This ... time ...

CYD

Oh, hey, Liz ... uh ...

LIZ

What is this?

CYD

I don't know.

LIZ

You don't know?

CYD

I don't know. He just came over and-

LIZ

Came over. What is this, Cyd? What did you do?

CYD

He came over looking for you and now here we are.

LIZ

What the fuck kind of answer is that?

She kneels next to SOME GUY.

Clark. Clark. Wake up.

She grabs his face and lightly slaps his cheeks several times.

Jesus Christ, how much did you have to drink?

SOME GUY starts to wake up. He is extremely groggy, disoriented and confused.

SOME GUY

Liz...

LIZ

"Liz", he says.

She laughs sadly.

God... what did you do?

SOME GUY

What?

He looks from LIZ to CYD and back again.

You're...

He looks down and sees that he's not wearing pants.

Oh shit... pants?

LIZ grabs his pants and throws them to him.

LIZ

Pants? Yeah, here are some damn pants. Put them on and get out of here.

He's very woozy and trying to get himself together in spite of it. He clumsily puts his pants on.

SOME GUY

Oh man... I don't know what—ughh—my head hurts.

LIZ

You need to go. I can't be in here with you; you need to go.

SOME GUY

What did I do?

LIZ

Go home, please. Just don't say anything.

SOME GUY

She did this. I don't know how, but she did this on purpose, I think … fuckin' bitch.

> *He staggers out the front door, mumbling. LIZ and CYD do not look at each other. LIZ starts to quietly cry. She covers her face with her hand. CYD gets up and puts on some pants. She goes up to LIZ and touches her shoulder.*

LIZ

Don't.

CYD

I'm sorry.

LIZ

You couldn't just let me have one thing?

CYD

It's not like that.

LIZ

You hated him from the start and you sabotaged our relationship. Because you were fucking jealous that someone else was important to me. God, what did you think- that I would thank you for it? Congratulate you for being so clever?

> *She's a mess, she starts clapping.*

Well done, Cyd. Really well done. I'm very impressed. We're all very impressed!

CYD

We shouldn't talk about this right now, you're angry.

LIZ

Do you think I'm going to get un-angry? Are you fucking crazy? I don't even know why I'm asking. You are fucking crazy. YOU ARE CRAZY!

CYD

I know. I'm sorry.

LIZ

You think if you just keep a cool head long enough I'll get over it. But I won't. I never will.

CYD

We'll be fine.

LIZ

No, fuck you. I can't even think of one reason why I would ever forgive you. I can't be your friend. There's nothing on my side of the fence. I give you everything you need and this is all I get back.

CYD

Come on.

LIZ

You're a God damn monster.

CYD

Hey, just ... well, stop acting like you came into this as my friend. Like you were doing everything out of generosity. You're my employee, after all.

LIZ

She starts laughing.

Are you kidding me? Do you have any idea when I last got paid? Do you have any notion of reality at all?

CYD

Sandy pays you every two weeks. She has all my financial stuff.

LIZ

Okay, let's just bring this out in the open right now: YOU'RE BROKE. You've been broke for a year.

CYD

What?

LIZ

You spent so much time and money drinking your God damn life away, that you apparently don't even recall that you don't exactly have an income anymore.

CYD

But I used to. I couldn't have used it all up.

LIZ

You did. That's how money works. If you use it and you don't make any more, it goes away. That's how everything works. That's fucking math.

CYD

The Dan Lennon show.

LIZ

Yeah, that paid a couple hundred bucks. That'll last about two more days.

CYD

Nobody said anything.

LIZ

I didn't think you could handle it. I made Sandy promise not to tell you. I don't even know what I was hoping for… I guess that you'd change, or… I don't know. I've been taking odd jobs at night when I know you won't need me anyway.

CYD

But you were still coming here.

LIZ

Because no one else would.

CYD

That doesn't make any sense.

LIZ

No, it doesn't. It doesn't make any fucking sense.

CYD

Then why did you-

LIZ

Because I didn't want to get a phone call three months later that your landlord had found your body, okay? So I showed up because I was your friend. Because I fucking cared about you. Because I loved you, for Christ's sake. God, how stupid is that? How stupid am I?

CYD

He was a shitty guy, Liz. He was a really shitty guy and now you know about it! We should be fucking… celebrating that!

LIZ

We're not talking about him. We're talking about you. You're a shitty friend.

                                CYD

Don't say that.

                                LIZ

You are a shitty friend.

                                CYD

You're the one with bad taste in people!

                                LIZ

You're a shitty person. Don't come near me. Don't call me. Enjoy the rest of your bourbon, you're just what it needs.

                                CYD

Wait! I didn't mean the employee thing. You just … you wouldn't believe me when I told you he was a bad guy. I had to show you.

                                LIZ

I cannot even begin to tell you how fucked up that is. What kind of friendship is that? Don't bother answering, because the answer is "the kind I don't want to have." okay?

                                CYD

I fucked up! I get it, I fucked up! I know that! You're right. You're always right. You're right about everything. I just … haven't you ever made a mistake?

                                LIZ

Not like this.

                                CYD

It can't cancel out everything else! All the good times. All the great times when things were really good!

                                LIZ

The great times?

                                CYD

When we'd go … get burgers! Or the times when my sets were really good or at least okay and you were there, and we'd get drinks and ride the subway and go the wrong way and fall asleep!

                                LIZ

You fell asleep. Because you were drunk. I stayed awake to make sure we could get home. To make sure YOU could get home. I'm always watching you sleep.

CYD

Or when we went to the movies! Or … God damn it, I don't know there were so many little times, Liz, when things weren't like this. Think about that, God, please think about it!

LIZ

I can't do that.

CYD

I'm sorry, okay? I'm sorry for everything I've ever done— every single thing! What can I do? Tell me what I can do!

LIZ

Take care of yourself. Be a person, for once.

CYD

I can't do that! Not without you here. You know I can't. You were right, I'll rot here alone. Liz, please. They'll find me dead, you know they will, you said it yourself!

LIZ

I have to go.

CYD

No.

LIZ

I'm going.

CYD

No. No. No. No. No. Don't say that. Don't leave me alone with myself.

LIZ

I wish I knew what it felt like to be in there. But I never will. And I'm not sure I could stand it. So I guess that means you're stronger than I am.

CYD

Don't.

LIZ

I'm outta here. I'm finally outta here.

CYD

Liz, you're all I have left.

LIZ

... I know.

> LIZ exits. CYD is left alone. She goes to the door and looks out, contemplating running after her. She doesn't. Instead, she sits down in the chair to think, and because now she doesn't have anything better to do.

ACT II

SCENE 6

> A bar with an open mic. CYD is CS on a stool once again, though she probably gets up and wanders at some point. There is a bottle of water on the floor.

CYD

So I am 30, which is a whole thing. I mean, once you're 30 it's like ... I'm just this now. Like, this is the best it's going to get until I lose my shit at 45 and start doing hot yoga in an attempt to reverse all the delicious damage I've done to my body. Here's a hot tip: don't look up who else is your age. Because you know who else is 30? Mark Zuckerberg. We are the same age. Let's just go through some little factoids here, for comparison. At 19, Mark Zuckerberg invented Facebook. At 19, I drank peach schnapps for the first time and threw a hockey skate at a man's head. At 23, Mark Zuckerberg became a billionaire. At 23, I did stand up on TV for the first time— which probably sounds pretty good— but it's important to note that on that same night, I ate a cookie off the floor of a bus, so ... make what you will of that. At the time, I thought it was chocolate chip, but recently I've admitted to myself that it was likely shortbread with something stuck to it. At 28, Mark Zuckerberg married a doctor. At 28 ... actually, I couldn't tell you what I did when I was 28. Maybe we can all look it up on YouTube later and see what sort of evidence we can find— or delete— or try to un-see. And now, at 30, Marky Z continues to study Mandarin, enjoys fried chicken pizza, and is learning how to cook, which is sweet. You know you've already accomplished too much if you're 30 and people care if you like fried chicken pizza or not. And what have I done so far, in my 30th year? I distinctly remember biting somebody ... and two weeks ago I did laundry for the first time. That is not an exaggeration. So, if you have tips about how to laundry, I will happily accept them. But I'm not on board for fabric softener, that seems like witchcraft. I'm trying to grow up, though. It's hard. I've only known one real grown up in my whole life, so I'm sort of making it up as I go along. For instance, as it turns out, grown ups don't usually sleep in the clothes they wore during the day. Or drink bloody mary mix for breakfast. Or have bottles of bloody mary mix scattered across their apartment so that they can reach breakfast whether they wake up on this side of the room, or the other! Also apparently they tend to wake up in a specific location in their apartment. This is all new to me. But I do okay. I do okay. Yeah, I do okay.

She looks down at her hand. It's shaking a little.

I don't know, does anybody really do okay? Are you doing okay? You don't have to answer that. Actually, you really shouldn't. Your own answer might freak you out and I don't want you to freak out in this bar, because then it'll be easier for me to freak out in this bar, and believe me when I say you don't want to experience that. You know, I used to know someone who … sorry, this isn't a joke. I'm just remembering something. It's okay if you don't laugh. She wouldn't.

She looks off to the side and nods.

I just got the light. That means I gotta go. Someone shines a light at you and it means it's time to stop. Some people see it and keep going, like assholes or really famous people. But I don't do that anymore. Shit, I haven't said anything funny for a while. Okay, how about just one more before I go?

She nods to the side at the person holding the light.

He says it's okay. All right, you know what would make flying way better? If Sean Connery was the pilot …

Lights fade out.

End of Play.

The Playwright

ALLISON PAGE has written numerous plays, including *Hellhound*, *An Historically False and Completely Imagined Lunch Date Between Misters Shakespeare and Marlowe at the Maiden's Head Pub For Aspiring Playwrights*, *Mrs. Youngblood*, *The Golden Apple of Discord*, and *April Showers*. Born in rural northern Minnesota, she moved to San Francisco in 2008. In 2010 she joined up with sketch comedians Killing My Lobster, with whom she writes and performs. Her non-dramatic writing has been featured in Women of Letters, Shipwreck, Write Club SF, Give Me Fiction, Travel Tavern and other scattered places. She wrote and performed in the two person shows Wegent & Page, Wegent & Page Draw The Line, and Wegent & Page Give It Another Try which was produced as part of the 2010 San Francisco Fringe Festival. As a performer, she's appeared in everything from *Prelude to a Kiss* to *Titus Andronicus* and can be found in various theaters in San Francisco when she's not writing at her desk.

More Plays From EXIT Press

Woyzeck, Pelleas and Melisande, Ubu Roi: translated by Rob Melrose
"Rob Melrose is a kind of magician, and his theater, Cutting Ball, is one of the most exciting and integrity-filled enterprises going in the sometimes-shabby field of the American theater. These translations, lucid and sharp, are a beautiful testimony to the value of Rob's achievement." — Oskar Eustis

Three Plays by Mark Jackson
"Playwright/director Mark Jackson has made his name as a first-class theatrical provocateur. Gutsy showmanship, brainy literary instincts and laser-sharp satire mark his canon." — San Jose Mercury News
The second collection of plays by Mark Jackson includes three plays based on incredible historic events: *God's Plot*, *Mary Stuart*, and *Salomania*.

Songs of Hestia: Plays From the 2010 San Francisco Olympians Festival
Playwrights Nirmala Nataraj, Bennett Fisher, Stuart Eugene Bousel, Claire Rice, and Evelyn Jean Pine adapt some of Western culture's oldest stories, illuminating our present-day concerns with imagination, creativity, curiosity and passion.

Snakes of Kampuchea by Mark Knego
A trilogy of plays about Cambodia, the Khmer Rouge, resettling into San Francisco's Tenderloin neighborhood, and returning to your homeland. Includes *Snakes of Kampuchea*, *Tual Kan's Journey*, and *Return to Angkor*.

EXIT Press is the publishing division of EXIT Theatre, a San Francisco theater company founded in 1983.   www.exitpress.org

www.ingramcontent.com/pod-product-compliance
Lightning Source LLC
Chambersburg PA
CBHW022305060426
42446CB00007BA/600